A Path of True Direction

Direction

A Journey of Faith

J.S. Peterson

Petey's Book Publishing

Preface

My heartfelt prayer is that these pages will match the deep desires of your heart. These pages provide you with insight, together with empowerment, which will direct you to achieve your purpose and find meaning and profound fulfillment. Your deepest longing should be to remember that God deeply loves you while also understanding your unique abilities and your purposeful destiny.

Deuteronomy 31:6

"Do not fear the road ahead, for God walks with you. His hand will guide you, and His grace will sustain you through every trial."

Introduction

B efore your first thought about God's presence, His divine plan for your existence was already written. God's unconditional love and divine authority demonstrate that His plan for your destiny existed before you were born. From the start, God orchestrated a heavenly plan that laid out your life's purpose and demonstrated His continuous desire to guide your path according to His divine will.

Has there ever been a strong, unending desire or a soft inner voice that led you toward something better? Your life carries a purpose that exceeds your present understanding. This book addresses the deep longing and inner understanding that reveals that your existence has a purpose beyond chance. The masterpiece represents a deliberate work of God in His vast story. Modern society tends to value short-lived indulgences and artificial accomplishments, which obscure the inner divine missions that exist inside our hearts. A special flame burns deep inside each person as a divine talent along with a passionate calling that waits to be set ablaze. The book functions as more than a self-help manual because it leads you toward discovering your divine nature and your life's divine purpose. Through personal reflections combined with theological insights and practical exercises, this journey will enable you to identify your God-given gifts while discerning His guidance so you can boldly follow the life He has planned for you. The call to action presents an invitation that leads you to fulfill your distinct role within the grand creation. You receive an opportunity to create a heritage that reaches past your passing. Are you prepared to start this transformative process of self-discovery? You are prepared to discover the extraordinary purpose that awaits you. Let's begin

Contents

Acknowledgements 171

Chapter 1

Understanding God's Unconditonal Love

To find your true worth, you must first understand God's complete love for you. The unshakeable foundation upon which a life of purpose and fulfillment is built. We need to understand our unconditional value to God before we can discover our God-given talents and listen for divine guidance because He sees us as progressing masterpieces rather than flawed projects.

This profound truth exists beyond emotional feelings because it forms the theological foundation that runs through scripture and empowers numerous people who find freedom and power in its message. The love that God demonstrates exceeds human understanding. The love God extends to humans does not function through exchange programs or achievement systems or require human accomplishments. The gift of divine love flows endlessly from God because it comes without conditions and continues eternally. The love transcends every failure and imperfection, and every doubting moment that we experience. The love of our divine Creator surpasses our imperfections to reveal the essential worth that resides within each person.

The parable in Luke 15:11-32 presents a perfect demonstration of boundless, unconditional love. The son functions as a symbol of human tendency toward misbehavior since he squanders his inheritance before living an unhappy life of inadequacy. When he returns to his father with repentance, his father chooses not to scold or ask for payment. His father receives him with full embracing love and celebrates his arrival through an extravagant celebration. A father's limitless love persists in waiting for his child's return, no matter what decisions the child makes in life. The parable contains more than heartwarming imagery because it reveals the fundamental nature of God's being. The story reveals the depth of his compassionate love and his unshakeable dedication to love. God's love stands unshakable in every situation because he shows us unwavering love even during our most unworthy moments. His love flows without restriction from our mistakes because

He gives it freely and abundantly in perpetuity, despite all our failures.

God reveals his boundless, unconditional love throughout all biblical writings. Romans 5:8 reveals God's love by showing us that Christ died for us while we were still sinners. God's love stands as a gift to us even though we remain in our state of sin. Salvation exists because of His love, which functions as its fundamental source rather than serving as an award for good deeds. His love exists before our worthiness and continues through every failure we make.

According to John 3:16, which stands as the most recognized Bible verse, God showed His love for the world by sending his only Son to provide eternal life to those who believe in him. This verse encapsulates God's love. The world received love from God even though it contained imperfections and sin. God provided His Son as the supreme sacrifice to create a connection between His divine nature and human beings. The love he shows extends into an endless and deeply selfless giving.

According to 1 John 4:10, the love of God is demonstrated through his sending of Jesus Christ to serve as an atoning sacrifice for our sins after he showed us his love first. This verse emphasizes God's initiative. His love emerged as an active grace that exceeded any possibility of human reciprocation.

His love extended to us before we found Him while we were lost and separated from Him without any deserving qualities.

People find it difficult to accept unconditional love because their understanding of worth comes from external sources. The way they determine their self-worth often depends on their achievements together with their relationships, and their outward appearance. People base their self-worth on cultural expectations while they pursue absolute perfection while avoiding criticism. A state of permanent anxiety develops from feeling always insufficient to meet others' expectations.

But God's love transcends worldly standards. His evaluation of our worth does not rely on our achievements or our mistakes. Through His eyes, we contain hidden potential and special beauty and divine purposes He has embedded in our hearts. God loves us because we are His dear children and His divine creation, regardless of our actions.

Unconditional love represents an intentional decision that goes beyond simple acceptance. We need to release the self-inflicted expectations of perfection and the need for external validation. We must let go of seeking endless approval while accepting our complete self, including our imperfection. The path to self-acceptance means we recognize that in spite of our imperfections we are loved by God even when we identify areas that need improvement.

Many people have learned to overcome their feelings of inadequacy after accepting God's loving embrace. The woman with the bleeding issue in Mark 5:25 experienced Jesus' compassion, which healed both her physical condition and her spiritual state. Jesus welcomed Zacchaeus, the tax collector, into his family despite the social exclusion he faced from others. The examples in these accounts demonstrate an established pattern that shows how accepting God's unconditional love transforms people's lives.

The path to understanding this love requires most people to progress over time instead of achieving it instantly. The process demands persistent work along with complete self-giving to God's gracious plan and complete trust in His divine guidance. We should engage in prayer together with meditation while studying scriptures that display God's limitless love. We must make a daily commitment to believe in His love even when our emotions or previous experiences and doubts attempt to convince us otherwise. We must learn to recognize our divine value through God's eyes because He loves us deeply and considers us precious. Our existence begins with this knowledge, which serves as the base for building our life of purpose. We can discover our individual gifts after understanding God's unconditional love for us. We already possess worthiness regardless of our accomplishments or perceived shortcomings. Our inherent worth exists as a divine gift that our creator provides to us without condition and maintains forever in the depth of their endless love. The unmovable truth will give you the strength to start your path with fearlessness, along with self-assurance, while understanding your genuine birthright value. This key serves as the entrance to discover a life of purpose, which leads to meaningful fulfillment that endures.

Chapter 2

Embrace Your Unique Identity

U nderstanding your inherent value stems from knowing that your worth is deeply embedded within your nature as a masterpiece of divine creation. The process of embracing your genuine identity becomes possible after you develop this understanding. This approach requires self-awareness that differs from narcissistic behavior because it means acknowledging your unique essence that God formed you to be. The process involves identifying your distinctive abilities alongside your natural abilities and your personal drive within God's larger plan.

Think of an orchestra. Every instrument, such as the violin, along with the cello, flute and trumpet, produces unique sounds which serve particular musical purposes. The orchestra contains instruments that produce melodies as well as instruments that generate harmony and provide rhythm. No instrument holds more importance than any other instrument because together they create the complete musical beauty and depth of music. Every person within God's creation possesses special talents and gifts that help form the perfect symphony. Each instrument brings its special contribution to the complete symphony rather than being considered a separate entity.

The knowledge dispels the broad societal mandate to fit into predetermined expectations of success and perfection. The media presents idealized versions of beauty together with achievement and happiness, which create feelings of inadequacy and self-doubt in people. We tend to look at others while wishing for their apparent achievements and while diminishing our unique capabilities. Our ongoing social media usage, combined with external validation fixation, causes us to experience both confusion and emotional emptiness alongside feelings of unworthiness.

However, God's vision transcends these societal constructs. Through individual evaluation, He observes our unique brilliance and potential that exists within each person. His purpose is to enable us to grow as distinct individuals by using the gifts He gave us.

The discovery of personal talents requires both prayer and introspection, together with attention to the Spirit's subtle directions. Identifying your gifts requires you to look at your passionate activities as well as your natural talents and achievements. What are you naturally talented at? What activities make you lose track of time? What problems do you want to solve? Your natural abilities usually reveal themselves through your natural aptitudes.

This process isn't always straightforward. Our natural abilities frequently hide beneath mental doubts and fears, together with the marks of previous experiences. We have silenced our personal aspirations because we assumed they were impractical and unreachable. We might avoid expressing our individual characteristics because we worry about what others will think of us. God's love gives us the strength to overcome these constraints. He expects us to be authentic rather than perfect.

The discovery of your distinctive nature takes shape over time while remaining a continuous process. People need to discover their strengths and weaknesses as well as their passions and potential throughout their entire lives. The process requires individuals to take chances beyond familiar boundaries to accept developmental possibilities.

It requires perseverance, resilience, and a willingness to learn from failures and setbacks. Remember, even the most accomplished individuals have setbacks. The key element is not the lack of failures but our reaction to them.

Embracing our distinctive selves demands that we eliminate the habit of comparing ourselves to others. The carefully selected moments presented on social media platforms tend to increase this tendency. We observe only refined versions of other people's lives while ignoring their difficulties and hardships. Through this process, we form an unrealistic view of reality that leads to feelings of inadequacy in comparison.

Furthermore, fostering self-compassion is essential. Show yourself the same care and understanding that you would provide to a close friend. You should recognize your imperfections and use mistakes as learning opportunities while permitting yourself to make errors. Self-compassion serves as a recognition of your inherent worth despite your flaws rather than self-indulgence.

God loves you because of who you are, rather than your accomplishments. Your existence in the world includes a unique life purpose that holds the power to create something essential for global society. Embrace your individual strengths while pursuing your passions and maintain your authentic self without fear. Your one-of-a-kind identity exists as a blessing that you should appreciate and develop while allowing it to illuminate for everyone to see. Your special contribution brings unmatched worth to the world.

This discovery journey towards self-acceptance exists without isolation. Your growth can be supported by family members and friends, and mentors who have faith in your abilities and want to see you succeed. Seek guidance from spiritual leaders and therapists, and trusted advisors who will provide support and perspective during your challenging times. Embracing your distinct identity requires navigating a complex path that contains both positive and negative experiences. Your final destination of purpose and authentic self-expression, and fulfillment makes every obstacle worthwhile. Face your life journey with both bravery and unwavering faith in your divine life purpose.

The obstacles we face while developing ourselves originate from internalized fundamental beliefs that we learned from our past experiences. We hear this message many times that we lack enough capability and intelligence, and talent. Such messages that are either directly said or hinted at through indirect language develop into internalized subconscious beliefs. Such internalization determines how we see ourselves while blocking us from embracing our distinctive qualities.

The process of overcoming limiting beliefs needs our purposeful assessment of them. This process requires us to challenge our negative self-talk by replacing it with positive affirmations through intentional questioning. We need to recognize the origins of these beliefs from past events, along with relationships and societal forces, before actively disengaging from narratives that no longer serve our needs. This process demands intentional work and dedication to challenge deeply embedded beliefs.

Your self-worth exists independently of what others think about you. Your worth exists within you naturally because God gave it to you. The thoughts of others should never decrease how valuable you are. Concentrate on your capabilities while developing your abilities and have faith in the divine destiny that guides your life, because your self-exploration shows God's creation as an irreplaceable masterpiece of life. Share your unique melody while your radiant essence illuminates the world.

Your process of self-empowerment through identity development continues throughout your life while you actively learn about yourself and embrace your entire self. The path requires you to dissect the multiple layers of your existence. Your divine essence reveals the exceptional gifts and talents that God created within your nature. The path leads to eliminating beliefs that restrict you and building confidence in yourself through gentle self-compassion. This path requires you to welcome your weaknesses while honoring your abilities until you discover your position in God's magnificent plan.

Remember that you always have companionship during your life journey. Your special value exists before God and a community of believers who will help you grow. Your faith and relationships with others and trust in divine life directions should be your foundation. Your self-identity stands as a valuable present from life. Embrace it, celebrate it, and let it shine brightly. Your unique contribution to the world is waiting to be revealed. Start your path of self-discovery to reveal the remarkable person God intended you to become. Your time has arrived to radiate your true self as the exceptional person God designed you to become. Your existence develops as a beautiful work of art, so you should fully accept its magnificence.

Chapter 3

Overcoming Limiting Beliefs

We must overcome our limiting beliefs in order to discover our true worth. These beliefs exist as hidden mental barriers that obstruct our ability to discover our divine life purpose while living out God's intended plan. These internal doubts whisper insidious messages that reshape our worldview, thus blocking our ability to fulfill the distinct mission God assigned to each of us. The narratives operate as powerful forces that shape our choices as well as our actions and determine our self-worth.

Where do these limiting beliefs originate from? Our beliefs from the past create their foundation. Our belief in inadequacy emerged from experiences with a critical parent and hurtful relationships, as well as repeated setbacks. The painful experiences have formed our perspective, but they do not

establish our identity. Societal pressures also contribute significantly. Our society maintains external validation as its main
focus while it forces people to compete against unattainable
standards of success and beauty. Constant comparison leads
people to doubt their own worth, which produces feelings
of inadequacy and self-doubt. We may experience doubts
about our spiritual identity through misunderstandings. Our
spiritual beliefs may become clouded when we doubt God's
love toward us because we feel unworthy and unlovable because of our past mistakes and perceived failures. We block
ourselves from experiencing God's complete love through the
self-imposed judgments we create.

We must examine our beliefs honestly while being willing
to face difficult realities in order to discover these restrictive
beliefs. The process requires us to explore within ourselves
to discover why we doubt our worth. The process requires
patience, together with self-compassion and a firm belief in
God's power to transform us.

We must challenge the validity of these beliefs once we have
identified them. These beliefs align with God's perspective
about us, or do they not? No, this is the definitive answer.
God extends unconditional love that is not affected by our
successes or failures, or by how we look or our known imperfections. Through His eyes, we have untapped potential

and unique value as well as an important mission to fulfill in the world. This knowledge serves as our defense against the destructive power of negativity that aims to engulf us.

The process of changing negative self-talk into positive affirmations serves as an effective tool for this transformation. We make a conscious decision to direct our attention toward our natural talents along with our God-given abilities instead of focusing on our perceived weaknesses. The practice of positive affirmations functions as strong spiritual statements that mold our subconscious thinking and develop our sense of value. The following statements demonstrate affirmations: "God loves me without any condition," "I am capable and strong," "I am uniquely gifted and talented," "I am worthy of love and belonging," and "God has a purpose for my life." Our minds transform through consistent declaration of these statements as they exchange unfavorable thoughts with optimistic faith-based perspectives.

The act of prayer stands vital in helping people overcome their beliefs that limit them. Through prayer, we can find God's comforting presence as well as His guidance and validation. The sacred space allows us to share our doubts and fears, as well as our anxieties, to experience His unshakeable love and assistance. The purpose of prayer reaches beyond requesting assistance because it enables us to welcome God's presence into our hearts so He can change our mindsets.

Scripture offers inspiration and affirmation. The process of reading and meditating on Bible verses that describe God's love and grace, and acceptance will substantially transform how we see ourselves. The Bible verse in Psalm 139:14 declares, "I praise you because I am fearful and wonderfully made; your works are wonderful. I know that full well," which helps us remember our special worth and God's detailed work in our existence. Our active study of God's Word helps us match our beliefs with His truth, which fights against negative thinking. Our complete understanding of our inherent value becomes stronger through this practice because such knowledge cannot be taken away by restrictive beliefs.

The process of overcoming limiting beliefs requires us to forgive both ourselves and others. Our refusal to release past grievances creates an environment where negative mental patterns continue to develop. The act of forgiving ourselves for previous errors lets us progress while liberating ourselves from guilt and shame that create obstacles for personal growth. Forgiving those who have caused us harm liberates us from harboring bitter emotions. The process enables us to free ourselves from anger and resentment, even though it does not justify harmful conduct from the past. The process requires us to select healing while embracing forgiveness.

Seeking support from others is essential. Our journey benefits from the support of family members and friends and fellow believers who create an environment of encouragement and accountability. The process of opening up about our struggles to trusted supporters allows them to both understand and validate our worth, which significantly helps us overcome feelings of loneliness and self-doubt. Supportive relationships give us a secure environment where we can work through our emotions while gaining fresh perspectives and finding motivation to keep moving forward. You are never by yourself as you walk along this path. God has intentionally placed individuals in your life to offer you support and guidance, along with encouragement.

Seeking help from a professional can be a valuable resource. A therapist or counselor brings effective strategies for managing negative thought patterns while teaching you healthy coping skills. Through their practice, they create an environment that safeguards our deepest wounds as well as helps us develop the self-compassion needed to break free from limiting beliefs. A pastor or mentor provides spiritual guidance to help you maintain your faith-based perspective while offering encouragement based on God's view of your worth. Seeking help demonstrates your strength instead of your weakness. Your dedication to personal development, along with your commitment to invest in your health, shows through this decision.

The last step involves acknowledging our achievements, no matter how minor they seem. Our tendency to focus on our failures leads us to disregard our accomplishments. When we make a conscious effort to recognize and honor our accomplishments at no size, they grow our self-efficacy and strengthen our confidence in our abilities. Our celebrations of successes help us redirect our attention from perceived shortcomings to our actual personal strengths, thus increasing our self-confidence and self-esteem.

The path of overcoming limiting beliefs extends throughout our lives as we dedicate ourselves to understanding ourselves better and accepting our true selves. The process demands unrelenting dedication and absolute trust in addition to persistent efforts to battle detrimental mental patterns. The rewards extend beyond measure when you live a meaningful life filled with fulfillment and genuine self-expression as the exceptional person God made you to be. Approach this path with bravery and faith and an unshakeable confidence in your natural worth. Your special voice and special contributions exist to be shared with the world. This is your time to shine.

Chapter 4

The Power of Self-Compassion

Our journey to understand our natural worth frequently encounters challenges. Our path toward growth often passes through areas of self-doubt under the influence of self-criticism we project inwardly. A persistent inner critic affects numerous individuals by continuously assessing their work and making negative comparisons while downplaying their achievements. Our God-given potential remains out of reach when perfectionism and fear of inadequacy fuel our inner critic to destroy our self-esteem. The hidden internal battle prevents us from attaining the life satisfaction that comes from following our divine life mission.

The pursuit of excellence represents the sinister nature of perfectionism. This apparently virtuous drive transforms into a destructive power that establishes unattainable expectations and views all failures as disastrous outcomes. The pursuit of flawless behavior leads to enduring dissatisfaction because it makes us believe we do not deserve love or acceptance or success. Our self-assessment against unattainable criteria results in an endless feeling of inadequacy. Our persistent drive for perfection simultaneously empties our vitality and drive while intensifying the internal doubts we seek to eliminate.

Perfectionism functions together with self-criticism to enhance our mistakes and flaws, yet minimize our achievements and positive traits. Our insecurities feed this behavior because it chooses to show our defects instead of our accomplishments. The critical inner voice speaks through harsh judgmental language, which repeats the negative feedback we received from our past experiences and cultural influences. These statements inform us that we lack both the necessary abilities and intelligence needed to succeed in life. The persistent negative emotions establish a destructive pattern of self-criticism that pushes us away from developing genuine self-esteem.

We must achieve freedom from this pattern through a complete mental transformation, which includes developing self-compassion. The practice of self-compassion stands distinct from both self-indulgence and passive acceptance of shortcomings. The practice of self-compassion involves active self-kindness when we suffer or fail or feel insufficient. We should extend the same compassion to ourselves that we would give to a close friend facing similar obstacles.

We must understand our connection to all people through the common experience of suffering and imperfection, and failure, which touches everyone. The moment we make mistakes, we should avoid hiding in self-reproach and shame because these mistakes affect everyone similarly. Through self-compassion, we become aware that our personal difficulties are not unique because others have traversed similar paths to become stronger, wiser compassionate versions of themselves.

Mindfulness serves an essential function for developing self-compassion. The practice of present moment awareness helps us watch our thoughts and feelings without judgment, which creates space between our inner self and our critical inner voice. Through mindfulness practice, we gain the ability to pause between negative self-talk moments so we can select a more compassionate response instead of acting on impulse.

Self-soothing methods serve as strong instruments to develop self-compassion. These methods require using our senses to create a soothing atmosphere. A warm bath together with soothing music and spending time in nature, and doing a favorite hobby represent potential self-soothing activities. These actions of self-care demonstrate our worthiness to receive comfort, which opposes self-criticism by providing self-kindness.

A person who experiences persistent self-criticism because of their inability to fulfill strict work requirements. They could practice self-compassion by acknowledging their work and the challenges they encountered and providing themselves with supportive words of understanding. I have done my best under difficult circumstances. I will extract lessons from this experience to improve my performance in future attempts. The practice of self-compassion transforms our way of thinking from self-judgment to self-growth and acceptance.

Self-compassion development needs active participation because it demands continuous, deliberate work. Learning to give ourselves kindness and understanding alongside forgiveness parallels how we treat our loved ones. The practice indicates inner strength because we have grasped the universal human connection while dedicating ourselves to personal growth. Through self-compassion practice, we establish an environment that supports our growth toward recognizing our natural worth and enables us to live with purpose and joy and fulfillment. Through self-compassion, we gain the strength and resilience needed to navigate life's journey by celebrating our achievements while learning from our failures with acceptance of ourselves. Our journey represents the unyielding divine love that reveals our intrinsic value even through our imperfect nature. The practice of accepting our complete self with all flaws becomes the foundation for living out God's magnificent life plan designed for each person. Through this challenging experience, we gain a better understanding of God's grace and our limitless capacity. Our everlasting strength and faith and hope, and self-compassion together demonstrate our lasting ability to transform through these divine attributes.

Chapter 5

Cultivating a Positive Self-Image

Our faith-based positive self-image grows through active selection of God's unchanging love as we see ourselves. The goal of this process consists of accepting our imperfections together with celebrating how God made us unique. The development of our faith-based positive self-image starts with shifting our perspective while we move from self-criticism to self-acceptance through better comprehension of our God-given worth.

Our self-image develops best through focusing on our strengths. The majority of us dedicate our time to our weaknesses while we both enlarge our flaws and reduce our achievements. Self-doubt arises from negative self-preoccupation, which stops people from realizing their complete potential. Our focus needs to be deliberately moved toward our natural talents and gifts, and positive qualities. Take some time for honest self-reflection. What are you skilled at? What do you enjoy doing? What are your passions? List them down. The small gifts which others might overlook hold value to God regardless of how insignificant they seem to us.

Review the accomplishments from your entire life, including both major and minor achievements. Did you overcome a significant challenge? Did you achieve a personal goal? Showing kindness or compassion to someone in need was one of your accomplishments. These accomplishments, which we often forget because of our self-critical nature, prove our ability to handle difficult situations along with our strong character and good heart. Reflect on these achievements during your available time. You should recognize your capabilities without self-boasting to appreciate your development. Writing them down can remind you of your accomplishments. Past achievements help people develop competence and self-efficacy, which both contribute to forming a positive self-image.

The practice of showing gratitude serves as an essential factor for developing a robust self-image. Gratitude directs our attention toward what we already possess while creating feelings of contentment and appreciation.

This practice helps us connect to God's providence in our lives while strengthening our belief that we are beloved children of God. Gratitude involves more than counting blessings because it requires us to recognize God's loving generosity toward us. Our awareness of God's blessings makes our faith stronger while demonstrating our true worth. The realization shows us we receive unconditional love from God because of who we are, rather than our accomplishments.

The connection between self-esteem and spiritual well-being, and purposeful living remains strong. Developing a strong self-image means both having confidence in ourselves and understanding our role in God's plan while living according to our divine purpose. Our self-esteem strengthens when we use our God-appointed talents and passions to live out our purpose. Our spiritual life creates nourishment for our self-worth by giving us comfort together with direction, and infinite affection.

In our purpose, we inevitably encounter setbacks and challenges. These difficult experiences provide us with priceless opportunities to grow and understand ourselves better. The manner in which we react to challenging situations determines the image we carry about ourselves. We choose to face our setbacks through self-criticism and despair, or we use them to develop new skills while trusting in God's guidance and strength. A positive outlook that identifies challenges as chances for expansion, helps develop a strong self-perception.

A professional career setback, such as missing out on a promotion opportunity, should trigger you to develop new competencies instead of self-attacks about your skills. Which skills, together with experiences, do you require additional development in? What are some strategies for enhancing your work performance? We should approach challenges with faith while demonstrating perseverance because God maintains his plan for personal development despite current circumstances.

A key transformative practice includes serving others through various forms of assistance. Our self-esteem experiences substantial growth through helping others through volunteer work and random acts of kindness, and simple support to people who need assistance. Our focus on other people's requirements makes us forget about our inner doubts and personal weaknesses. Through acts of service, we gain awareness of our ability to love and care for others, which helps us develop a sense of value beyond our personal accomplishments. Through selfless action, we connect with something greater than ourselves, which brings life enrichment and strengthens our self-image.

Furthermore, self-care is essential. The practice of self-care represents more than indulgence because it means sustaining our physical as well as emotional, and spiritual health. Engaging in activities that bring us happiness and calm, such as nature time and hobbies, and mindfulness practice, strengthens both our spiritual core and our sense of self-worth. The practice of self-compassion shows our dedication to self-care since it demonstrates our value and care for ourselves, which is vital for building a positive self-image. By making self-care a priority, we enhance our physical and mental health while developing stronger capabilities to love ourselves and others.

The powerful image of a blooming flower should be contemplated. A flower needs sunlight and water, together with nurturing soil, to flourish, while human beings need nourishment to develop a positive self-image. The divine sunbeam of God's love shines constantly on each of us. Water symbolizes self-compassion, providing the necessary hydration and sustenance. Our faith community, along with loved ones, acts as the nourishing soil that supports us. When we actively maintain these life elements, we create the perfect environment for our self-image to grow and expose the divine beauty and strength God has given us.

Constructing a positive self-image demands ongoing personal development and self-understanding. The development of a positive self-image needs ongoing dedication along with self-compassion and absolute faith in God's unshakeable love. Accept your path while honoring your triumphs and studying from your failures because you carry within you the natural right to love and receive acceptance and find fulfillment. Your true value exists independently of your accomplishments or how others view your flaws. God gives you this gift, which reveals itself as a shining truth deep inside you while you await complete recognition. Trust in God's life plan so your self-image can mirror the amazing person God intended you to be. Trust in God's endless love while you embrace your journey and celebrate your strengths.

Chapter 6

Recognizing Your Spiritual Gifts

We have built our faith-based positive self-image, yet now we need to discover our spiritual gifts. God gives us unique abilities which form his divine plan to serve His kingdom while achieving His life mission for us. Using your spiritual gifts leads to more than personal happiness since it enables you to join God's universal plan for humanity.

Each person's process to identify spiritual gifts represents an individualized and complex experience. Your spiritual gifts discovery process requires both an authentic self-examining mindset and the ability to recognize your natural abilities and recurring meaningful experiences that point to divine purposes. Such exercises demand real inner contemplation and prayerful attention to the Holy Spirit's direction.

This spiritual practice demands more than casual exam-
ination because it needs deep self-examination along with
prayer and divine inspiration. You should investigate which
activities lead you to deep happiness and serenity. The tasks I
perform with natural ease and skill are what? The situations
that keep returning to my mind have a particular pattern that
signals to me a divine mission.

The spiritual path requires prayer to be an essential component for seekers. Seeking God's wisdom and guidance represents the main purpose of prayer instead of requesting gift
revelation. Find peaceful silence to let the Holy Spirit light
your path. Devote yourself to seeking God's revelation of
your special talents and His plan for their use to bring honor
to His name. You should read sacred scriptures with prayerful attention to discover both your divine purpose and your
divine potential. Listen to the Spirit's guidance because He
provides insights through sudden epiphanies and meaningful
scriptural verses, and strong inner convictions.

Trusted individuals can offer important outside perspectives through their feedback. The people closest to you, such
as family members along with friends and spiritual mentors and church leaders, should be consulted. You should
ask them to evaluate your abilities while highlighting your
accomplishments and instances where your actions created

positive effects on those around you. Their observations will both validate your gifts and help you understand them better through objective evaluation. To receive genuine feedback, you must select people who share your trust and provide meaningful comments instead of empty compliments. Open your mind to their observations regardless of whether they expose aspects you might not have recognized. Their views tend to expose your hidden abilities that you cannot easily see in yourself.

The gift of service expresses itself through ordinary acts of kindness that people show to others in their normal daily relationships. People with this gift recognize the requirements of others and respond with caring actions. The way they operate in life escapes observation from others, but their actions create significant effects. People with this gift provide forgiveness and compassion to others during difficult moments. The gift of empathy, together with perspective understanding, usually accompanies this ability even when others have caused damage. Those with the gift of giving often help those in need. The gift requires more than financial assistance since it includes the generous use of time along with effort and resources.

The spiritual ability to heal exists as one of God's gifts. Physical healing is not the sole requirement for this gift, although it could be included. Emotional healing and spiritual support are key components of this gift. The gift includes providing comfort to those who are suffering while leading them toward peace and consolation. This gift enables someone to automatically feel the pain of others while providing comfort and hope. Administration as a gift means to arrange resources and coordinate events, as well as direct tasks. A group setting benefits from this skill because it increases efficiency and enhances collaboration. This essential capability supports the smooth organization of teamwork while maintaining productive outcomes.

People who demonstrate leadership skills naturally inspire others to work together toward achieving shared objectives. People with confidence and vision achieve their goals. This person can recognize hidden strengths in others while working together effectively and developing team cohesion. The practice of hospitality requires more than event planning. A welcoming environment should be created for others while providing them comfort and value. Your duty should be to connect with people who feel isolated and lonely while creating a sense of belonging that encompasses everyone. Spiritual gifts identification continues throughout your entire life while you learn and discover new aspects of your faith. The more you use your gifts to serve God and others, the clearer your true calling will become. You will encounter situations where you lack certainty or demonstrate inadequacy. This is perfectly normal. Trust that the Holy Spirit will guide you while you listen to feedback from others and stay committed to using your divine gifts. Your global impact is substantial because your abilities are precious and you are essential to God's divine arrangement. The awareness of these gifts fails to determine your value as a person. Such a recognition demonstrates our appreciation for God's gifts and His love towards humanity. All gifts become powerful tools for community development and God's kingdom expansion when they are used in faith.

These gifts present themselves either clearly or quietly to the human perception. Your spiritual gifts will reveal themselves to you through time as your faith and self-awareness develop. God's plan will reveal itself through His grace and time, even though you might not see all your gifts right away. To find your spiritual gifts, you need to walk by faith and seek guidance through prayer and self-reflection, and by asking for help from others while maintaining humility. Let your unique gifts grow and flourish through God's service and his service to others. Your actions will leave enduring effects throughout the world. God's love is boundless, and His grace is abundant, and your gifts are vital to accomplish His plan.

Chapter 7

Overcoming Fear of Failure

Our God-given talents need to be unlocked and used while facing various anxieties, with fear of failure being the most challenging one. This fear, which occurs to every human being, becomes especially intense when we plan to devote ourselves to something we feel has divine approval. The voice delivers poisonous questions that create detailed images about possible failures and public embarrassment, together with useless work. This fear stops us from using our abilities, which causes our gifts to remain inactive while our capabilities remain unachieved. What if we transformed our fear into a transformative force instead of allowing it to stop us? We should understand that failure functions as a pathway to achieve success rather than an ending.

Our understanding of failure needs to undergo a complete transformation in order to adopt this new perspective. Our thinking should transcend the basic opposition between achievement and non-achievement. We should acknowledge that talent development consists of many accomplishments alongside numerous failures. The process of learning incorporates failure as an essential component, which teaches valuable lessons to those who choose to learn. The process of stumbling and making errors and facing apparent failure creates opportunities to reflect while you analyze and make necessary adjustments. The process reveals which parts of our skills need improvement so we can develop better strategies that result in stronger abilities.

The foundation of this comprehension exists deeply in religious faith. The foundation of our confidence should be built upon our belief in a loving God who supports us, thus allowing us to meet challenges with bravery and strength. Scripture shows numerous cases of people who endured severe challenges in their lives, but God does not guarantee a trouble-free existence. Through faith and determination, these individuals developed into stronger, wiser individuals who grew closer to God. Through their experiences, people learn about the transformative effects of facing obstacles. The biblical accounts of Joseph and David, and Jesus himself, demonstrate how faith combined with resilience leads to victory after enduring deep challenges. The historical narratives demonstrate methods to handle our personal life challenges by delivering motivational wisdom to those who fear failure.

We should challenge our fear of failure through a complete assessment of what success actually means. The external world determines success through recognition and material achievements, along with public acknowledgement. Although these outcomes bring positive results, they should not determine our sense of accomplishment. The development of God-given talents requires an inner growth process that combines personal development with knowledge acquisition and self-exploration. Our mission involves using our talents to benefit others while creating beneficial change across the world without needing external rewards. Moving our attention toward personal development eliminates the power that fear of failure holds. Setbacks become opportunities for refinement. We direct our efforts toward striving for excellence while focusing on the ongoing development of our journey rather than seeking perfection.

Several real-world methods exist to help people overcome their fear of failure. The process of dividing challenging work into smaller sections makes the entire task seem less overwhelming. This method enables us to recognize and enjoy minor achievements during the process, which helps keep us motivated while boosting our self-assurance. Every finished stage in our work helps us recognize our advancement, which strengthens our faith in our capabilities and future success. The process of mountain climbing becomes manageable when we focus on reaching individual landmarks while appreciating the views at each new location.

The development of a growth mindset plays an essential role. We should welcome challenges because they present valuable chances to learn new things rather than treating them as dangers. People should recognize that their abilities exist within a developmental range that grows stronger through focused practice. A change in perspective enables us to view failures as educational experiences that provide essential guidance for future decision-making. The process of failure demands that we learn from errors while we improve our methods and continue forward despite failures. Another important action toward overcoming fear of failure includes the process of seeking feedback. Hearing constructive criticism may be challenging, but it delivers precious information about areas where improvement is needed. The ability to refine our talents exists as a precious gift that leads to better performance and boosts our chances of success. A crucial factor exists in selecting the proper source of feedback. Select people who both support you and give you useful guidance and comprehend your objectives. Through their observations, you will discover unknown weaknesses and learn how to tackle obstacles better.

Remember the power of prayer. Keep your faith strong throughout this entire path. Pray for guidance, strength, and courage. Seek God's help to defeat your fears while he reveals your special direction in life. Through faith, we receive unshakeable backing which enables us to handle unknown situations and stay strong during tough circumstances. Faith offers comfort along with encouragement and a constant reminder that you possess value as a child of God.

Finally, embrace the process. The path will contain instances of self-doubt, together with feelings of frustration and obstacles that will arise. Our development, along with our growth of resilience, leads us to discover the complete potential of our gifts through these challenges. Honor the entire journey while recognizing the wisdom gained and new abilities developed, and personal growth achieved during this time. Your value comes from following God's divine mission even when faced with fear and unknown circumstances. Your life path showcases your religious dedication along with your bravery and God's eternal affection, which granted you special abilities for a vital mission beyond your individual needs.

Chapter 8

Turning Talents Into Action

After discovering your God-given talents, you need to transform them into practical achievements. True faith emerges through this process, which takes discovery and self-awareness into actual service. The goal is to use God's blessings to carry out His will as well as assist other people. The main goal of this process is to fulfill God's purpose while creating a meaningful impact on the world and achieving deep happiness from living according to His will.

The initial step toward turning talents into action involves actively searching for chances to apply them. To achieve this goal, you need to demonstrate proactive behavior while pushing past your comfort boundaries and actively seeking divine guidance to find appropriate service opportunities. The first step should be to pray for clear guidance and understanding.

Ask God to show you where your talents will produce the greatest effect while He also reveals the paths that fit His plan for your life. The prayerful approach functions as an interactive divine partnership that brings God's wisdom and guidance to your decision-making activities.

Examine your natural gifts to determine their potential to benefit others. For example, if you demonstrate natural aptitude for teaching, volunteering at a local school or church would be appropriate. Do you possess writing abilities? You should start by writing for a church newsletter and then expand to create devotional articles and establish a blog to spread your faith messages across various readers. Your musical abilities represent a gift from God. You should use your musical talents by performing in church events and community musical presentations, and composing worship music. The possibilities are vast and varied, limited only by your imagination and willingness to step forward.

Small acts of service carry tremendous strength in their ability to create positive change. Every minor service that seems unimportant now can start a chain reaction to create beneficial outcomes that honor God. Your service through talents reveals God's love by performing acts of kindness and offering listening and helping hands. Use your talents to generate happiness and assistance, and motivation for all individuals within your social circle, including family members and friends and neighbors and members of your community. Some of the most impactful contributions appear as unobtrusive actions.

Use your talents to enhance your professional work beyond traditional volunteer activities. You should look for work in fields that match your abilities and your personal interests. Your current role may require creative approaches to integrate your natural abilities. Your organizational talent should help you optimize workplace operations to enhance productivity and decrease work-related tension. Your strong communication abilities would make you an excellent link between different departments or teams. Seek opportunities that enable you to use your gifts to deliver mutual benefits to your employer and yourself. Your work achievements will simultaneously meet your spiritual and professional objectives.

The inability to find opportunities to use your talents should not discourage you from seeking. Your failure to recognize opportunities indicates you must enhance your understanding of your gifts, together with their appropriate applications in the world. Self-reflection and mentorship from spiritual advisors, and acquired skills acquisition can help you advance your self-understanding. You should enroll in educational programs or participate in workshops and self-study activities to improve your talents, which will expand your available choices for serving others.

The process of discovering talent-based opportunities continues beyond a single occurrence. Your personal growth leads to talent development, which creates fresh possibilities. Maintain an open mind for new prospects and maintain flexibility in your methods of operation. You should maintain flexibility in your plans by adapting them as needed while seeking divine guidance throughout your decision-making process.

Using talents for action requires individuals to handle the obstacle of judgment or rejection. The fear intensifies when you attempt to do things beyond your familiar territory. Pursuing goals that matter to us. Your value exists because God created you as his beloved child, and no one else has the power to define your worth. God provided you with these talents for a special reason, and He will provide you with the needed strength, along with the courage to accomplish them, regardless of how others react.

The fear of failure should not stop you from moving forward. Look at failures as chances to develop your knowledge while improving your abilities. Your progress toward your goals and your determination to succeed will both develop through every life experience you have. Use your mistakes to acquire new knowledge while developing better strategies before continuing to pursue your God-ordained purpose.

The importance of community support should always be kept in mind. Find people who support you and provide positive feedback as well as practical guidance because they believe in your abilities. The pursuit of ambitious goals will encounter inevitable obstacles, but a strong support system provides invaluable assistance during these times. The support network you should have includes your family members and friends, together with mentors and spiritual advisors, along with fellow believers from your faith community. Share your dreams and aspirations with them and let them celebrate your successes and offer encouragement during times of difficulty. Their support will strengthen your resolve and help you maintain momentum on your journey.

In your quest to fulfill God's plan for your life, remember to take care of yourself. Your ability to sustain energy and maintain a positive outlook depends on maintaining proper care for your physical body and emotional and spiritual health. Make time for activities that bring spiritual nourishment while keeping yourself anchored to reality. Taking time to rest and recharge and spending time in nature and doing hobbies, and practicing mindfulness or meditation can be part of this process.

Keep your focus on the long-term while acknowledging each achievement because they demonstrate your faith and dedication to follow God's will. Use your talents to serve God and create positive change while celebrating your path, drawing wisdom from errors, and focusing on the ultimate goal of bringing glory to God.

The journey of converting your talents into action continues without interruption as you face both obstacles and advancements. Give yourself time because spiritual development takes place at a slow pace. There will be times when you feel overwhelmed, frustrated, or even tempted to give up. During these times, remember the importance of prayer and seeking God's guidance. Place your faith in God while trusting in His plan, which guides your life journey. Allow Him to strengthen you, renew your resolve, and guide you on the path He has designed for you. The talents God has given you exist to benefit the world, not just for your individual advantage. Your talents stem from God, yet they exist for purposes that surpass your personal needs, so receive this duty with both gratitude and service-minded humility and dedication. Through your God-honoring service of talents, you will gain personal satisfaction, yet you will simultaneously benefit the world at large. Your efforts will create a lasting impact that goes beyond your death. Your unique contribution to the world, combined with your faith and actions, will serve as a demonstration of God's blessings and your dedication to His plans for your existence.

Chapter 9

The Importance of Prayer and Meditation

After demonstrating why people should turn their divine gifts into actual accomplishments, we need to discuss fundamental tools that help this process: prayer and meditation. These religious practices serve as essential ways to connect with divine guidance instead of being mere religious rituals. These practices enable people to understand God's will and obtain the wisdom needed to fulfill their life purpose. Prayer and meditation establish the fundamental elements of building a relationship with God. This partnership gives us the strength to follow God's plan in life.

When practiced in its most basic form, prayer functions as an ongoing dialogue between humans and God. Prayer consists of more than just asking for things because it represents an active exchange of ideas, thoughts and emotions and intentions. Through prayer, we expose our hearts to God while revealing our vulnerable moments along with our victories and doubts. Listening to His soft whispers becomes possible through this practice when you are amidst all the noise of life. Most individuals experience difficulty with effective prayer because they feel uncomfortable or lack clarity about expressing themselves to God. God seeks authentic communication with you rather than flawless verbal expressions. Start by speaking with God in the same manner as you would communicate with a reliable companion. Express your heart's concerns to Him, then thank Him for His blessings while asking for direction throughout your daily schedule.

You should create a regular time for prayer as part of your daily schedule. Spending only five minutes devoted to prayer can create significant change. Choose an area where you can avoid interruptions while you dedicate your attention to God. You can pray at any time, such as when you wake up or right before your day starts or during your lunch break or before going to sleep. The essential quality of consistency leads to a stronger bond with God while developing a deeper relationship through regular practice.

Prayer exists beyond both formal prayer locations and traditional prayer rituals. You can speak to God about your life experiences whenever you encounter challenges or experience joy, or spend time reflecting. Your spontaneous dialogue with God builds stronger bonds between you and Him and maintains your divine connection all day long. You should maintain a dialogue with God during your normal activities throughout the day. You do not need to do this, but you can use it to improve your bond with the divine.

Prayer serves as a fundamental tool with meditation, to help people receive guidance from God. Meditation requires more than mental emptiness because it develops profound awareness to let divine presence fill your entire being. A space of quiet contemplation enables you to hear the Spirit's whispers. Through meditation, you can hear divine guidance by tuning into its frequencies and silencing external noises.

Different meditation approaches exist. Guided meditation brings comfort to some people who use audio recordings and apps that lead them to relaxation and contemplation. People who prefer silence choose to meditate by concentrating on their breathing patterns or a chosen visual object. Through this method, their thoughts become peaceful while their spiritual essence establishes a bond with God. You should try multiple methods until you find the method that works best for your needs.

A successful method requires choosing a personal word or phrase that holds significance to you. A personal mantra functions to stabilize your mental and emotional states. A mantra can be either a scriptural verse or a hymn verse, or a basic term such as "peace" or "love." When you silently repeat this word to yourself, it enables you to silence your internal thoughts while reaching deeper states of consciousness.

Visualizing a peaceful scene or a meaningful image stands as an efficient method for achieving effective meditation results. Visualization can be either a natural environment or a significant memory, or a religious emblem. The practice of immersing yourself within this image creates mental peace, which enables deep contemplation. The act of focusing on one specific image helps to silence mental distractions so you can reach divine connection.

The main goal of meditation techniques is to establish mental clarity while focusing on the present moment. The silent environment provides you with the ability to connect with God more deeply so you can gain knowledge and obtain divine directions. The purpose of meditation allows you to stay present while you hear God speak His blessings. The goal is not to clear your mind perfectly but to make room for God to communicate with you.

Regular practice constitutes an essential element for both meditation and prayer. Begin by meditating for 5-10 minutes until you reach a comfortable duration. Consistency is essential. Your relationship with God becomes stronger through meditation practice, while it also improves your ability to understand divine guidance. Consistent prayer practice combined with meditation leads to improved divine connection, which results in increased insight and spiritual guidance.

We need to approach meditation and prayer with both openness and humility. We need to recognize our inability to guide ourselves while recognizing our complete dependence on God's direction. The main purpose of prayer and meditation is to surrender to God's will by trusting His plan for our lives. Our goal should be to follow His purpose while seeking His wisdom and allowing Him to lead our actions.

God's presence and guidance become more apparent to us when we establish deeper connections with Him through prayer and meditation. We develop the skill to hear His voice above worldly distractions so we can detect His direction in our everyday activities. Our intuitive guidance system develops into a strong directional tool that guides us through life's challenging situations to select paths that fulfill God's purpose. The longer we practice prayer and meditation, the more distinctly we will hear God's voice, which will lead us toward our special life mission.

The spiritual practices of prayer and meditation serve as fundamental tools that help us achieve our purpose and achieve satisfaction in life. These practices allow us to reach the divine realm and gain wisdom while converting our divine gifts into useful services that benefit God and our fellow human beings. We begin a transformative path by maintaining steady prayer practice and meditation practices. Through prayer and meditation, we uncover our personal life mission together with our essential role within God's universal plans. Through faith and action, empowered by prayer and meditation, we find deep satisfaction and deep meaning in our lives. Our divine purpose becomes clear after listening and learning, which results in a life that follows God's plan exactly. The path unfolds as we listen, learn, and act, constantly seeking guidance and deepening our relationship with the Divine.

Chapter 10

Seeking Wise Counsel and Mentorship

The process of obtaining wise advice along with mentorship remains essential for understanding God's guidance. The messages God delivers through intuition and dreams and circumstances, and relationships become clearer when we receive guidance from others who share their wisdom and experience. Faith exists mainly in community because believers provide each other with support and both guidance and tests that help spiritual growth.

A skilled climber who guides beginners through a difficult mountain climb serves as an analogy for this situation. An experienced climber provides directions that include warnings about dangers and specific recommendations for successful ascent. In the same way, spiritual mentors provide essential guidance to lead people through the difficult paths of their life's journey. Their knowledge helps create a framework to understand God's communication methods. Such guidance enables us to recognize actual spiritual revelations from our personal prejudices, along with outside worldly interruptions.

Selecting an appropriate mentor stands as a critical decision. The ability to deliver reliable spiritual guidance does not exist in all people. Select people who display the qualities you wish to see in yourself. People who want to mentor should demonstrate an enduring faith commitment, and their actions should match both their personal beliefs and biblical standards. You need a mentor who will promote your development instead of creating dependency. A mentor who provides genuine guidance helps people learn to discern independently while giving them the necessary tools to interpret God's guidance. A true mentor helps you discover your answers instead of giving direct solutions.

The responsibilities of mentors go beyond delivering guidance to their mentees. The mentor will keep you responsible and provide directions when needed, as well as mark your achievements with support. A mentor establishes a protected environment to welcome openness about your doubts and fears and personal struggles without any form of criticism. A supportive environment stands as the essential foundation for spiritual development because it enables you to thoroughly evaluate your experiences while discerning God's will without imposed expectations.

You can locate such individuals in what places? You should begin your search by looking at members of your church and your family, along with professionals in your network. Look for people who show spiritual development alongside thorough biblical knowledge and active religious practice. These individuals may be found among pastors or elders or teachers, or regular members of the church community who have followed a similar spiritual path. They can offer wisdom gleaned from personal experience.

Mentorship requires you to take initiative when asking for their counsel and guidance, while not merely accepting their opinions without question. Present specific questions to your mentor that relate to your current problems and choices. Show your mentor all your situations, including your religious practices and your dreams and the events surrounding your difficult decision. A mentor will not direct your actions, yet will assist you in hearing God's message. Their knowledge will expose unknown flaws while defining

God's guidance to you and direct your actions toward His divine plan.

The mentoring process delivers advantages that transcend the present moment of guidance. Through their mentorship, they teach essential Christian practices such as prayer and Bible study and self-reflection, which build up a strong faith. They provide access to beneficial resources while linking you with supportive people and enabling you to develop a solid spiritual community. A mentor typically serves as a model who shows you how to practice faith in real life and teaches you to blend religious principles into your personal relationships and work, and community service. Their prayerful dedication, together with their responses to difficulties and their service activities, show how faith transforms into real action. Your path will become more compelling because of this.

The experience of seeking mentorship brings the same level of self-discovery as the mentorship process itself. Humility and recognition of your personal boundaries, along with a willing attitude toward receiving direction from others, define this process. You should take deliberate steps to identify mentors while showing them your need for spiritual guidance and proving your dedication to developing this relationship. The search for mentors requires some experimentation since not every candidate will match your needs, and it is perfectly fine to look for multiple mentors, throughout your life. The essential factor is to locate someone who delivers wisdom that aligns with your spiritual development.

Mentorship operates in two directions. Your mentor provides valuable wisdom and experience, yet you provide reciprocal value to their guidance. Through your insights and questions, and personal experiences, you deliver new perspectives that enhance the spiritual development of your mentor. The spiritual growth of all parties involved should occur through respectful and learning exchanges and shared dedication to spiritual advancement.

You need to dedicate time to discovering other available perspectives. Your primary mentor can provide vital support, but expanding your mentorship network to multiple mentors with distinctive abilities will deepen your knowledge while expanding your viewpoint. The spiritual growth of a person becomes more complete when they have mentors who specialize in family life and careers, as well as ministry. A diverse set of mentors who bring different life experiences will help you understand God's guidance better in different situations.

The process of finding wise counsel and mentorship continues throughout your spiritual development because your requirements will shift while your mentoring connections may transform. Seek mentorship at different stages of life because your relationship with mentors should evolve with your personal growth. Your continuous search for wisdom demonstrates your dedication to following faith throughout life. Your wish to live in accordance with God's plan becomes visible through this behavior. The quest to receive and give guidance continues throughout our entire lifetime as individuals and through the wisdom of others. Spiritual growth becomes more meaningful through this pursuit while enabling us to achieve our divine life purpose. Start this journey with humility and eagerness, and keep your heart receptive to God's loving guidance. Spiritual growth through this essential practice will yield many more blessings and insights than the time you invest.

Chapter 11

Trusting in God's Timing

The spiritual path presents trusting in God's timing as one of its most difficult elements. Our modern society emphasizes the importance of obtaining quick results along with swift progress and immediate fulfillment. The natural rhythm of God's intervention in our lives runs at a different speed than the rush of modern times. Our search for His guidance and our prayers and obedience to His directions remain dedicated. We face various challenges during our spiritual journey, which include delays and setbacks as well as times when God seems uninvolved. Such circumstances create discouragement while also leading to feelings of frustration and doubt. We need to understand the method to preserve our faith while God operates at a different pace than us.

The foundation of this answer consists of developing deep faith in God's sovereign control and his perfect timing. Active faith represents a profound trust that recognizes God possesses unlimited wisdom and power and infinite love. The understanding reveals that He possesses complete awareness of everything, including our situation, better than we do, while uniting all things to create benefits for us (Romans 8:28). This understanding enables us to shift away from our restricted viewpoint so we can accept His plan even when we fail to grasp its meaning.

The Old Testament account of Joseph presents an important lesson to us. Joseph experienced years of slavery followed by false imprisonment after his brothers sold him into slavery. During his prolonged suffering, Joseph kept his integrity while trusting in God's divine purpose for his existence. Through his unshakeable devotion during extreme challenges, he rose to become the ruler of Egypt. His leadership saved his family, together with numerous other people, from the famine. Through Joseph's experience, God demonstrates His ability to transform adverse situations into beneficial outcomes according to His exact schedule. God uses negative events to create positive results that emerge at His perfectly timed moments.

The purposeful nature of God's timing remains essential to understand because His decisions follow a deliberate plan. God uses the events in our lives to refine our faith while building its strength and equipping us for what lies ahead. Every obstacle we face during the waiting period creates opportunities to develop spiritually and build character, and understand God's love more deeply. The time we wait allows us to learn patience and develop resilience as we grow in dependence on Him. Through waiting, we also obtain the chance to develop new abilities as well as knowledge and forge important relationships. These skills will be essential to fulfilling God's purpose in our lives.

To follow God's timing, we need to abandon our personal wishes and objectives. We tend to handle our spiritual journey with an urgent mindset while seeking to guide the direction of outcomes. Many believers establish particular timeframes they want their lives to unfold while setting definite expectations about their future and preferring specific routes. Our refusal to let go of expectations stops us from discovering God's genuine intentions. The path He chooses might differ completely from what we had in mind. True trust requires letting go of our own expectations so we can accept God's divine will. We know that His plans surpass ours and His understanding surpasses our understanding (Isaiah 55:9).

A deliberate choice to surrender our lives for God's purpose stands as a fundamental aspect of this process. Such decisions remain true regardless of whether we must postpone our desires or encounter short-term difficulties. Our purpose is to seek His guidance actively while trusting in His wisdom and staying obedient to His instructions. This occurs even though the future remains unclear to us. Our belief needs to focus on God's beneficial plan regardless of our present understanding. Our faith grows stronger through dedicated prayer and Bible study and by depending on the Holy Spirit.

A positive outlook becomes essential during the time we wait. The practice of ignoring problems or pretending all situations are perfect does not qualify as this attitude. We select to concentrate on God's unwavering faithfulness and His goodness, together with His unbreakable promises, while facing challenges. The practice of gratitude for existing blessings enables us to trust God's provision of future needs. Our positive attitude enables spiritual strength, which helps us keep our attention on God's eternal love and constant presence. Our ability to withstand life's challenges becomes stronger while we stay firm in our religious beliefs.

The practice of trusting God's timing becomes stronger through the presence of a community. We should seek support from loving friends, along with family members and believers who will encourage and keep us accountable during our waiting periods. By disclosing our problems and fears to people who understand us, we obtain relief from our troubles and discover new reasons to have hope. Seeking wisdom along with guidance from trusted mentors and spiritual advisors provides priceless insight, which helps people make better decisions. Our spiritual mentors motivate us through times of discouragement while showing us God's faithfulness and assisting us to maintain our focus on what matters most.

The time spent waiting for God to fulfill his plan brings about regular experiences of impatience, along with frustration and doubt. These feelings are normal and shouldn't be suppressed. Spiritual health demands that we process our emotions truthfully both through prayer and by sharing them with trusted people. During these moments of vulnerability, we encounter God's grace and compassion at their deepest levels. Our efforts to share our problems help us solve them while bringing encouragement to people who go through comparable struggles. The practice allows believers to give support to each other while enhancing their mutual understanding.

Trust in God's timing represents an expression of faith because it confirms our belief in His sovereignty and goodness and His love. The path requires patients who remain steadfast in their search for divine guidance. The path toward divine alignment will test our patience, but God promises infinite benefits to those who submit to His plans. Through trusting His exact timing, we will find peace along with His presence while receiving the fulfillment that comes from devoting our lives to His loving plan. God's timing appears mysterious to us, but it remains perfectly divine. Every experience in life leads to our highest good because God guides us toward a destiny that surpasses our most optimistic dreams. Our destiny exceeds all expectations, although we must endure detours and unanticipated delays. The path leads us toward spiritual growth and deeper faith in God while revealing His endless love and divine grace. Our complete experience of His purpose together with His love becomes possible through waiting while surrendering to trust in His divine plan.

Chapter 12

Understanding Your Unique Calling

The search for your specific life purpose extends beyond finding happiness in your professional work or individual targets. Our being connects to a divine purpose that surpasses our individual existence through this process. The journey of self-discovery merges with spiritual enlightenment while we seek to match our personal gifts to God's worldwide mission. The mission exceeds job searching since it involves discovering your distinctive impact that both represents your spiritual essence and creates enduring change for all of humanity.

People usually mistake their divine assignment with their occupational path. Career fulfillment plays an essential part in one's calling, although it does not represent the complete truth. A career functions as both a professional occupation and a financial source and an outlet for skill application. Your calling represents a deep inner purpose that guides you. You have a fundamental feeling that God wants you to fulfill a particular mission that matches your core values and natural abilities and produces positive change in the world. This distinction is crucial. Your career provides financial stability and brings personal contentment to your life. Calling reveals an inner meaning beyond personal achievements because it allows you to find your place within a greater whole.

You should view your professional life as performing on an instrument, but your divine mission involves creating musical masterpieces. Your instrument, whether violin, piano or guitar, demonstrates your natural abilities. Your symphony represents the unique masterpiece you create to share with the world. It's the only melody you can create. Through your gifts, you create a unified symphony that expresses your individuality. Your spiritual beliefs, together with your strong passions and understanding of divine plan, shape the symphony you create. This way of life emerges through deliberate action while being guided by profound life meaning and purpose.

What methods enable us to discover our individual divine life mission? Each person must experience this process individually, and it typically develops through gradual self-discovery stages throughout their lifetime. Such realizations emerge gradually through time rather than through immediate epiphanies. People need to observe themselves, pray, analyze their life events and actively listen to God's subtle guidance.

Reflection of your passions and talents serves as a strong method to find your calling. What are you naturally drawn to? What activities make you feel truly alive and engaged? Do you possess particular abilities or talents that people value or benefit from? These indicators usually reveal the special talents God has given you for your unique mission. These activities surpass pastimes because they present opportunities for your divine calling to emerge.

The discovery of your talents needs to be combined with religious devotion and prayer practice. Your path to God's purpose will become clearer through regular prayer and biblical reflection, and seeking guidance from spiritual mentors. Through prayer, we become receptive to God's directions while He reveals our path ahead. Through regular scriptural engagement, we gain understanding of God's personality together with His plans and learn from those who dedicated their lives to following their divine assignments throughout time. Spiritual mentorship from mature believers provides essential guidance, along with support and wisdom, to those who seek it. Through this process, you will learn to recognize God's direction in challenging life situations.

You must observe your life situation together with available opportunities. The experiences of life, together with our difficulties and connections, serve as tools which God uses to develop and perfect our life mission. Those apparently random occurrences that people view as barriers or failures may actually function as vital indicators of your special life direction. Stay receptive to unanticipated changes in your life path. Through unexplained processes, God guides people through unexplored territories to discover their definitive life purpose. Trust His exact timing and leadership as you accept the journey, even when your path remains unclear.

Discerning your calling requires a process of trial and error. You will explore different paths as you try various opportunities while also facing setbacks. These obstacles should not discourage you from proceeding. Look at these challenges as learning moments that help you develop your understanding of your spiritual gifts and abilities. Each life experience, including failures and successes, provides essential understanding which clarifies your special life path.

The spiritual path of your calling transforms as you develop spiritually, and your knowledge of God's plan becomes more mature. The journey of a lifetime continues without end as a journey rather than a final destination. Maintain flexibility while being open to fresh possibilities that match your growing faith. Your spiritual connection to God leads to a deeper comprehension of your divine mission. The path evolves through your spiritual development and faith experience.

Living according to your life's purpose demands both faith and perseverance, along with courage. The path of your God-given purpose requires you to move beyond your comfort boundaries and encounter obstacles while taking bold risks. Pursuing your life purpose leads to infinite rewards that go beyond measure. Your divine purpose brings you a deep sense of accomplishment, together with stronger divine bonds and the reward of making significant impacts on the world. The fulfillment that comes from knowing your divine mission exceeds all earthly achievements because it gives you inner peace that results from carrying out your assigned role in God's design. This spiritual path requires unwavering dedication and persistence, yet it demonstrates God's miraculous transformation power.

God has specifically designed your calling to be individual and unique based on your personal experiences and spiritual gifts within his divine plan. Self-discovery and spiritual growth form the foundation of this deeply personal journey that avoids generic approaches. Your life becomes a distinct

composition that you play in the grand symphony of existence. The melody you create enhances the divine musical
arrangement of God. Follow your spiritual journey by listening to divine messages so you can understand the significant
impact God has planned for you to make on the world. Your
contribution matters. Every person possesses a life purpose
that can be revealed through discovering their divine calling.
Trust in both the process and God's timing so you can start
the extraordinary journey of realizing your distinct life purpose.

Chapter 13

Setting Goals Aligned with Your Purpose

Your understanding of passions and gifts and their potential intersections that direct you toward life purpose should be turned into practical goals. The process demands more than a vague wish for future alignment with your divine calling because you must establish a specific plan to pursue God's intended life path. Achieving purpose-based goals needs people who can see the big picture, along with practical thinking and absolute trust in God. The achievement of your life goals requires understanding the complete picture alongside the necessary smaller steps to achieve it.

The first natural response would be to create broad, extensive goals that seek rapid change. Setting an ambitious goal creates more frustration than beneficial results. Unrealistic goals tend to cause both discouragement and burnout as their result. The solution consists of developing a systematic series of achievable milestones that drive continuous advancement. Think of it as building a cathedral. The entire structure should not be lifted into place simultaneously. Instead, place one brick at a time. The methodical approach maintains both momentum and hope throughout the process.

A person who understands their life's purpose to study and teach theology needs to consider their next actions. The ultimate goal for this individual involves getting their theological work published and securing a seminary teaching position. The expansive goal represents a noble yet challenging objective that surpasses immediate reach. The goal demands fragmentation into multiple achievable parts. The initial step toward this goal demands the writer to produce monthly chapters that concentrate on theological education aspects. The next step involves researching seminaries while finding potential educational programs. Networking with accomplished theologians while seeking their guidance should be the third step. The individual steps toward the goal allow you to experience success, which motivates you to continue moving ahead.

The biblical practice of sowing and reaping matches the process of dividing complex objectives into workable portions. Your faith-driven actions when you diligently work at each step create fertile ground for God to nurture. Through consistent efforts at seemingly minor actions, you will harvest substantial accomplishment and fulfillment over time. The journey of faith requires steady progression while trusting God's direction instead of rushing to reach the destination immediately. The journey itself brings substantial value to the process because it creates chances for spiritual development along with educational and personal growth.

The goal-setting process demands a thorough assessment of your available resources that exist in both physical and non-physical forms. Your time, along with your financial resources and your access to tools and materials, make up your tangible resources. Your resources also include your skills and knowledge, together with your support system and your most vital resource, which is faith. Your assessment should be honest about your capabilities by distinguishing what you can accomplish independently and what needs additional work or external backing. A theologian in development would require additional theological education and better writing abilities, and connections within theological communities. The overall plan requires you to integrate these essential components.

The process demands recognition of possible hurdles followed by development of strategies to overcome them.

What challenges might arise along the way? How can you prepare for them? Anticipating potential difficulties enables you to create backup strategies that protect your advancement. A theologian starting their career may encounter writer's block alongside publisher rejection and monetary limitations. Creating strategies in advance for anticipated challenges will help you defeat them while keeping your main objective in focus.

The process of setting goals requires regular assessments and evaluations to achieve success. Periodic evaluations should take place to check your advancement and modify approaches while acknowledging your accomplishments. Your continuous assessment enables you to adjust your approach while staying responsive to environmental changes. Your goals will stay true to your developing purpose and God's life plan through this approach. The reflective practice serves dual functions of evaluating progress and obtaining guidance to determine your upcoming journey directions. You can find both clarity and direction through prayerful reflection to confirm that your efforts follow God's will. The power of prayer should never be minimized during this transformative process. When you establish your goals, make sure to ask God for His guidance along with direction. Ask for wisdom, strength, and perseverance. You should invite the Holy Spirit to shine light on your path, which will give you both clarity and understanding. Prayer extends beyond help requests because it creates an intense bond between you and God, who performs His divine plans in your life. The continuous dialogue between you and God plays an essential role in maintaining faith and hope when you encounter obstacles or begin to doubt.

Remember that setbacks are inevitable. The occasional setbacks and disappointments should never stop you from pursuing your established path. Use setbacks to learn new things and develop as an individual while modifying your strategies and exploring alternative viewpoints. The combination of persistence along with complete faith will enable you to defeat challenges on your way to achieving your targets. Every obstacle you face strengthens both your faith and your ability to persevere.

Make sure to celebrate all your successes, no matter how small or significant they may be. Recognize your achievements and show gratitude to God because of His leadership and support. These celebratory moments restore your vitality while intensifying your determination and reconfirming your dedication to your life's path. The celebrations strengthen the positive feedback mechanism, which motivates additional advancement and validates your selection of direction. Your path to God's fulfillment will become possible through the combination of consistent progress and faith together with perseverance.

Chapter 14

Overcoming Obstacles and Challenges

Life's purpose journey tends to avoid linear progress. You should anticipate taking wrong turns while facing unforeseen barriers and encountering complete route closures. This experience marks neither failure nor success because it exists as an essential part of your journey. True resilience and strengthened faith emerge when we learn from failures and continue moving forward despite adversity.

The most prevalent challenge people encounter is doubt. Doubt enters quietly through our minds with harmful ideas about the unclear purpose of life and useless work, and impossible achievements. Multiple factors, including fear of failure, together with external criticism and perceived lack of progress, can create these doubts. The solution against doubt exists in absolute faith that embraces God's life direction regardless of uncertain directions. Your faith should be an active trust in God's direction, although the complete picture remains unseen.

Faith development needs the practice of developing robust spiritual routines. You can develop faith through daily prayers and meditations, along with studying the Bible and participating in religious activities that feel meaningful to you. Your faith becomes stronger through spiritual practice, which gives you access to the divine power and wisdom needed to handle doubts and obstacles. Prayer acts as a weapon that fights doubt while affirming your faith because it represents your active search for divine guidance.

Fear stands as another major challenge that people encounter. The strong emotions of failure, fear and unknown fears act as powerful barriers that stop us from advancing. Fear causes people to procrastinate and avoid tasks and refuse to take necessary risks. The process of overcoming fear requires awareness of its presence, followed by the deliberate selection of faith over fear. The process does not require ignoring your fears, but requires both acknowledgment and understanding of their origins before taking action despite them. A person who feels called to start a ministry serves as an example. The prospect of public speaking combined with financial unpredictability and potential failure creates a state of overwhelming fear. Through faith and continued prayer, a person can acquire the strength needed to defeat their fears and proceed. Trusting in God's guidance and provision allows you to move forward.

Financial constraints are another common challenge. The path to realizing your life's purpose typically demands financial resources, yet economic instability creates substantial stress, which blocks your advancement. The economic aspects of your mission-focused career change or educational pursuits, or business establishment require thorough planning and financial analysis. God provides for us in ways we cannot predict. Trust in His provision, seek financial guidance, and develop a realistic budget. Search for additional revenue streams that can help increase your income. Financial boundaries should never determine what you do or where you go. Creative thinking, together with prayer and planning, enables people to overcome this barrier.

External criticism and discouragement are also inevitable. Your selected journey will not find approval from every person in the world. Several individuals will doubt your decisions, along with numerous others who will doubt you and some who will make deliberate efforts to discourage you.

The negative comments of others should not determine what your purpose in life truly is. You should direct your focus toward the divine guidance along with the affirmations from your trusted network of support. Other people's negative words should not dim your faith or your resolve. The doubts they express originate from their own beliefs and restricted understanding rather than any assessment of your potential. Numerous biblical figures maintained unwavering faith while facing intense opposition, which demonstrates how important perseverance and faith are when dealing with adversity.

When someone demonstrates both passion and drive, they risk encountering burnout as a major challenge. The deep dedication needed to achieve your life's purpose creates physical and emotional exhaustion. The identification of burnout indicators along with specific prevention measures constitutes an essential requirement. Establishing boundaries while practicing self-care alongside scheduled relaxation becomes necessary for everyone. Regular exercise combined with healthy eating and sufficient sleep, together with mindfulness practices, will help you achieve balance while stopping burnout from occurring. Remember, you cannot pour from an empty cup. Your pursuit of purpose demands proper care for your physical state as well as emotional health and spiritual well-being. Devoting specific periods to rest while reflecting and renewing yourself must be included in your daily routine. These practices represent fundamental building blocks for maintaining a lasting journey rather than being optional treats.

Progress becomes severely affected when you face health problems. Sudden illnesses, together with accidents, create physical restrictions and emotional suffering, along with monetary expenses. Address your health first by obtaining medical care and using your network for support during challenging times. These challenges exist temporarily because your life purpose continues to guide you. Seek guidance and support from both the medical and spiritual communities. You should incorporate faith elements into your healing process by recognizing that healing is a divine plan. View challenges as opportunities for growth, reliance on God, and increased appreciation for your blessings.

A solution to these obstacles needs multiple strategies to overcome them. Reflection through prayer requires you to ask God for direction and strength during this time. Consult trusted mentors along with spiritual advisors and members of your faith community for guidance and support. Their wisdom, combined with their encouragement, creates priceless help when times become challenging. Professional counseling might be beneficial to consider since therapists offer essential tools that help you handle stress while conquering fear and building your resilience.

Fear and discouragement, together with doubt, will appear at times, yet they represent short-term challenges only. Accept every test that comes your way while gaining knowledge from them, while keeping your ultimate target in mind. Your life's purpose follows a spiritual path that leads to personal growth and spiritual discovery while maintaining prayer as your guide. Each obstacle you overcome strengthens your faith while building your determination, which enables you to handle upcoming difficulties better. Your journey will reveal itself as a source of powerful strength and blessing as you persevere. The true prize comes from the changes you experience in your life's process rather than reaching your objectives. Trust in God's plan while embracing your journey through faith and unwavering determination.

Chapter 15

Integrating Faith Into Your Daily Life

Daily faith integration goes beyond adding religious rituals to your schedule because it requires infusing spirituality into every aspect of your existence. We need to identify God's presence in both significant life events as well as in ordinary daily activities like preparing coffee and traveling to work, and spending time with family and work colleagues. The integration between faith and daily life develops into a flexible spiritual connection that maintains an ongoing dialogue with God.

Prayer serves as a fundamental instrument for people to connect their faith with their everyday activities. Prayer consists of more than memorized words because it represents an intimate dialogue between ourselves and our Creator, which forms a spiritual connection. The space provides a platform to acknowledge every blessing, no matter how big or small, which adds value to our existence. During times of crisis, people find comfort and strength in prayer, which helps them navigate their challenges. Through prayer, we can obtain direction and wisdom as well as discernment to handle the intricate nature of life.

Prayer's beauty lies in its simplicity. A formal setting and elaborate rituals are not necessary for this practice. The ability to communicate with God happens silently throughout our active day or through deep, heartfelt expressions during evening tranquility. The essential aspect lies in developing a regular practice of divine engagement. Set aside daily time for specific prayer practice by using guided meditation or reflection techniques. The deeper your connection with God becomes, the more your prayer transforms from a scheduled ritual into spontaneous spiritual encounters.

The practice of prayerfulness can extend beyond traditional prayer periods into our daily activities. To maintain awareness of God's presence, we should keep Him in mind during every activity we perform. Our daily work tasks should begin with awareness of their spiritual value because our actions matter to God. Before making any decision, we must seek God's will, then request direction to align our choices with His divine plan for our lives. The ongoing mindfulness between us and the Divine leads to a stronger bond, which converts ordinary tasks into religious practices.

To integrate faith into daily life, it is crucial to study Scripture. Christians view the Bible as an active living document that provides wisdom along with guidance, and inspirational power. A devoted study of the Bible enables us to comprehend God's nature as well as His sacred promises and divine plan for our future. The practice of faith receives nourishment from this study while our determination grows stronger, and we gain better tools to handle everyday difficulties. The study of Scripture requires personal engagement with its content to let God's Word communicate directly with our hearts.

Bible study can take various forms. Reading brief Bible passages each day while thinking about their spiritual meaning for your personal life is one possible approach. Bible study with fellow believers through small groups allows meaningful discussions about the sacred text. Through the use of commentaries and additional resources, one can conduct a detailed textual analysis to achieve a better comprehension of the scripture. Choose a study approach that suits your preferences and establish it as a regular practice. The purpose extends beyond knowledge acquisition since God's Word has the power to reshape both our spiritual and intellectual understanding.

Integrating faith into daily life requires seeking God's guidance in all our everyday choices beyond Bible study and prayer. The purpose of this approach is not to get divine answers for all everyday situations but to acquire wisdom for vital decisions that match our spiritual beliefs. We should pray to God for both understanding and power, and bravery when making choices that follow His plan. Our dedication to His life mission constitutes the second part of this requirement. The practice of seeking God's wisdom requires us to stop our activities while reflecting, praying and seeking spiritual guidance.

We should consult with trustworthy mentors or spiritual leaders in such situations. We should take moments of silence to determine which path would be the most suitable. We should analyze the different possible results from each decision through the lens of our spiritual values and principles. Our search for God's guidance in decision-making strengthens our faith and directs our decisions toward our life purpose.

The practice of integrating faith into our daily professional activities faces various obstacles. The pursuit of living according to our faith creates difficulties when we try to maintain our integrity while resolving ethical issues and building relationships with colleagues. We discover authentic living through these specific obstacles. The workplace demands that workers bring compassion together with integrity and service to their duties. Our workplace requires us to treat colleagues with respect and kindness, even when conflicts arise. Seeking justice and fairness stands as our responsibility in all our interactions. Our mission is to shine like a light in darkness while spreading hope throughout a world filled with skepticism.

We need to incorporate faith into our relationships to achieve our purpose in life. We need to provide others with compassionate understanding and empathetic treatment. God's grace and mercy should be extended to others through forgiveness because He has shown us mercy first. Healthy relationships need our care while we build solid foundations of trust and support between people. We should work on reconciliation by handling conflicts through God-honoring methods that build stronger relationships. We should understand that God created every person in His divine image, so we must show them honor and respect in our interactions.

Our leisure time serves as a time for integrating faith into our regular activities. We can develop closeness to God through various activities. Listening to inspirational music alongside reading spiritual literature and attending religious services represent some ways to achieve this goal. Our time should be used for helping others through acts of service, which combine our abilities with volunteer work for those who need assistance. Devoting time to nature allows us to observe God's beautiful creations. We should dedicate our leisure hours to spiritual development by strengthening our bond with God while reaffirming His mission for us.

The process of integrating faith into daily life continues indefinitely instead of reaching a final goal. The journey demands continuous work with deliberate practice while submitting to God's divine plan. The path requires us to accept our flaws and trust in God's guidance throughout the journey. Our goal should be to demonstrate faith through our actions as much as through our words. Faith should permeate all parts of our existence so we can become instruments through which God accomplishes His divine purpose. Integration of faith functions beyond being strict rules because it represents a living relationship that develops through faith, hope and love.

Chapter 16

Building Supportive Relationships

S upportive relationships function as a religious requirement that establishes the basis for living a purposeful existence. The path to achieving our divine mission rarely exists
alone. We exist as relational beings because God created us
to belong to community networks. Faith-based relationships
create a system of support that helps people handle obstacles
while enjoying their achievements during this journey.

Support isn't about cheering. Authentic support requires
individuals who share common values alongside mutual respect, along with dedication to personal growth. We need
people who support our faith path through their understanding and validation so they can provide help in difficult

moments and monitor our progress when we deviate from our path. These relationships create an environment that allows us to reveal our weaknesses while sharing triumphs, while remaining shielded from criticism.

The process of finding supportive individuals demands both self-reflection and spiritual guidance for discernment. What people in your life consistently boost your spirit and push you toward growth while keeping you true to your core values? The supportive people in your life could be your family members or close friends, together with mentors and other members from your faith community. The people who stand by you throughout your journey will support your achievements and provide solace in difficult times while maintaining your God-designed direction.

To establish such relationships, one needs to be purposeful. Supportive individuals will not appear by themselves, so we need to take the initiative to build these connections. To build these relationships, we must proactively search for them by maintaining dedicated relationships with sincere concern. Your church membership or faith-based community offers a potential path to building connections through small group involvement. Your passion for a cause can guide you toward volunteering while participating in activities that match your values. Engaging in important dialogues with others while practicing attentive listening alongside sincere motivational words.

These relationships need complete accountability because of their critical value. Pursuing your purpose with a supportive community means you join a united group that strives together for a common objective. The joint responsibility creates both the necessary framework and drive to keep going through difficulties and mark achievements. Through accountability partners, you will gain direction as well as help to overcome delays and maintain your dedication to your goals. Your support network provides essential guidance at critical moments by offering both motivation and guidance alongside performance evaluation for your objectives.

Through these relationships, we take on joint responsibility that goes beyond individual duties. Through supportive relationships, people work together to achieve their common mission.

A faith-based community with purpose values helps its members develop an intensified awareness of shared goals. Our individual work becomes essential to God's worldwide mission because we belong to His purpose.

Mentoring is essential in developing supportive relationships. Experienced individuals who have traversed similar paths offer precious wisdom, together with direction and motivation to those seeking guidance. A mentor will explain potential obstacles ahead and teach methods to deal with them, and offer support during confusing times. The process of mentorship allows both knowledge acquisition from others and knowledge sharing of personal experiences. To find mentorship, one must demonstrate both humility along a willingness to gain knowledge from people who have come before you.

Religious relationships need active forgiveness to grow strong in faith. We all make mistakes, and sometimes those mistakes hurt the people we love. Our decision to maintain resentment and anger creates destruction in our own lives as well as damage to our connections with others. Christian forgiveness allows us to free ourselves from resentment and emotional pain, which block our healing process and spiritual growth. The decision to choose love along with reconciliation stands as a better option than the choice to hold onto anger and resentment. Through forgiveness, we obtain liberty, which enables us to advance into new relationships built on strength.

The immediate advantages of support and encouragement from strong relationships help people overcome inevitable crises and difficult situations in life. Life brings inevitable storms, which include both unexpected difficulties and unanticipated failures and unexpected obstacles. Strong relationships give us the strength to face life's storms so we can discover comfort and power in times of hardship. Our faith community functions as a sanctuary that provides comfort and both spiritual and practical support to its members. The development of strong supportive relationships requires constant effort, together with empathy and genuine care throughout an ongoing process. We must develop our connections through forgiveness while showing grace to others, just as God has shown grace to us. People need to make purposeful time investments for developing deep discussions and cooperative experiences, and mutual backing. We must actively look for ways to meet new people and maintain availability to help others when they need it.

Our relationships mirror our faith-based values alongside our commitment to our faith and our goal of leading an important life. Through these relationships, we gain empowerment to move forward on our journey during times of challenges and failures. These relationships serve as both physical and mental resources while representing our dedication to a faith-based life of purpose. Our active construction of supportive relationships builds a faith-based community network that strengthens our faith-centered lifestyle by turning personal challenges into community achievements and helps us stay true to God's purpose.

Chapter 17

Embracing Challenges as Opportunities for Growth

When we embrace challenges that appear impossible to overcome in life, we do not deny their painful nature or deny their existence. The practice involves changing our perspective toward difficulties by focusing on personal growth that can occur directly within challenging circumstances. This is a vital foundation for developing a life that serves its purpose. At such crucial times, our faith becomes tested while our resilience grows stronger and our understanding of God's plan becomes more profound.

Our faith becomes one of the essential spiritual teachings we discover when facing difficult circumstances. Surrender is not weakness; it is a profound act of faith, a conscious decision to relinquish control and trust in God's plan, especially when we cannot see the path ahead. We understand that human knowledge fails to grasp what God intends. The practice recognizes that His work takes place despite all our suffering and confusion. The process of surrender requires an active decision to put our trust in God's power above our own abilities. God's light exists even when we experience our most challenging nights.

The act of surrender requires us to release our preconceived plans and expectations and our attempts to determine final results. Our lives have been meticulously planned, and we have worked hard to establish clear goals which we have pursued diligently. Our well-arranged life plans get interrupted by challenges, which reveal our inability to manage everything and push us toward accepting the unknown future. The opportunity to grow emerges exactly when we surrender our inflexible plans and allow God to direct us toward a new journey.

The acceptance of challenges demands the development of a resilience mindset. Our ability to bounce back from difficulties and learn from mistakes while persevering through hard times defines resilience. The development of inner strength becomes possible when we learn to face challenging periods without losing our faith or hope. Spiritual practices such as prayer, meditation and scripture study enable people to develop resilience, which builds through regular practice. These spiritual practices help us acquire both strength and serenity, which enables us to handle tough situations with composure.

When confronted with difficulties, we should analyze them through religious beliefs by asking: "What valuable lesson can I obtain from this circumstance? What lesson does God want to teach me? Through which actions can I convert this obstacle into a deeper spiritual connection with God?" Our attitude of inquiry during difficult times helps us turn adverse situations into meaningful spiritual understanding and individual progress. Opportunities to learn from difficulties rarely appear straightforwardly, and obtaining their lessons requires significant effort. Prayer combined with reflection and guidance from spiritual leaders and wise mentors allows us to understand God's reasons behind our challenges.

We acquire knowledge from our challenges through spiritual insights and concrete methods to defeat obstacles. A person must believe in God's will while actively working to resolve their problems. To successfully overcome challenges, we need to conduct an authentic self-assessment to determine our abilities and weaknesses before seeking assistance when needed. We should look for guidance from experienced counselors and mentors, or therapists, to help us deal with our difficulties.

The process of overcoming adversity reveals talents and skills that we did not know we possessed. We discover unknown reserves of bravery along with tenacity and innovative thinking, which challenge us to develop these skills. The new abilities we discover will turn into essential tools that drive our future growth and achievements. Overcoming challenges builds our character while deepening our faith and increasing our capacity to show empathy and compassion.

Our perception must transform into gratitude when we see problems as chances to develop ourselves. We can develop gratitude through the blessings that exist in our lives when we focus on them, even though we face difficult situations. The practice of gratitude does not reduce the intensity of hardships nor their difficulties. Our attention moves to beneficial aspects when we adopt this perspective, which shows us that light exists even in dark times. Practicing gratitude builds our spiritual strength so we can meet challenges with purpose and hope.

Life takes us on a path of continuous progress, yet it includes many obstacles and difficult moments. We can use challenges to build spiritual and personal development by understanding them as transformative opportunities. We overcome challenges through surrender and resilience, together with learning and seeking help and discovering our hidden strengths and practicing gratitude. Our journey reveals that faith transforms us into stronger, wiser individuals who deepen their connection with God and discover their life purpose. The power of faith demonstrates its transformative abilities through my life experiences as God maintains his grace even during times of storm. Every obstacle functions as an opportunity to grow. The path leads us toward better comprehension of ourselves and our faith while revealing our future purpose. Your faith develops through challenges, which simultaneously help you become a better person.

Chapter 18

Service to Others Leads to Discovering True Joy in Life.

The deep peace and contentment we create by practicing gratitude exist to be shared with others. Our heart and hands naturally extend to help others after this inner peace flows from our spiritual practice. The act of serving others creates a meaningful pathway toward spiritual growth, which delivers life-changing fulfillment. Our giving produces returns in the same way that natural systems operate through cause and effect. The rewards from material blessings are not the primary result of this practice. Our souls undergo deep spiritual growth while our faith becomes stronger, and we develop profound connections between God and people through this practice.

Serving others has many blessings. Serving others directs our thoughts toward external matters, so we stop worrying about ourselves. Our preoccupation with helping others usually leads our personal problems to fade into the background. The new way of thinking delivers an essential break from our continuous mental discussions that exhaust our energy and decrease our happiness. Our freedom from personal preoccupations emerges when we serve others, which results in mental liberation.

Service to others gives us a concrete method to display our faith. Our beliefs function as more than theoretical beliefs because they require expression through real-world activities and relationships with other people. Our religious beliefs find their true manifestation in serving others, through which we transform our beliefs into tangible demonstrations of love and compassion. Our divine connection grows stronger through our faithful actions, which lead to a more meaningful spiritual path and reveal our life's purpose.

Helping others creates joy because it directly aligns with the fundamental nature of our human existence. Through divine creation, we received our image and acquired empathy along with compassion and love. We possess these attributes as active gifts that require development through expression and sharing with others. The act of serving others enables the divine qualities within us to grow while bringing joy to those we assist and ourselves. Each act of service we perform helps build our capacity for love and compassion while strengthening these qualities.

Service requires effort and understanding that the process will be challenging sometimes. We will experience difficult moments along with emotionally exhausting and demanding situations. The genuine test of our resilience and compassion emerges from facing these difficulties. The difficulties we face reveal to us what true sacrifice and love, along with empathy, really mean. The benefits that come from serving others exist beyond immediate reward or measurable outcomes, yet they create enduring and powerful results. These experiences form our character traits while building our spiritual bond with a force that exceeds our personal existence.

We can provide service to others through multiple channels. The requirements for grand gestures or heroic acts do not apply to this situation. Ongoing small gestures of kindness performed with genuine love create substantial effects in the world. Listening to friends who need help and helping neighbors, and volunteering at local charities, along with donating to meaningful causes, all make up effective methods to serve others. The small actions we perform create a positive effect that expands into the world to touch numerous lives, including our own. These collective acts of service build up our community structure and develop a strong spiritual bond with faith.

The advantages created by our service reach past the people we directly assist. Our efforts to serve others frequently bring us unexpected presents. Our own lives become richer because of the gratitude we receive from those we help, along with the sense of community and purpose and deep connection we establish. This beautiful exchange proves the deep connections between all human beings while showing the power.

A spiritual dance between giving and receiving constitutes the practice of selfless giving. The spiritual process of giving and receiving creates an endless flow of blessings that enhances the spiritual growth of both individuals.

Service to others enables personal growth. Our individual growth happens through venturing past comfort zones to encounter new challenges that push our limits. These experiences enhance our resilience, adaptability, and capacity to empathize. Our acts of service enable us to discover new knowledge while we develop ourselves better and understand our place in the world. Our personal transformation improves both our service capabilities and our ability to find joy, along with achieving peace and fulfillment.

Our connections with others become stronger when we dedicate ourselves to serving others. Intentional service acts performed with compassion strengthen bonds between people while building mutual respect and appreciation. A shared purpose creates an essential support network that enhances our lives through collective work toward common objectives. Working together creates a sense of community that develops essential relationships while forming new ones. People find life's complete fulfillment through their relationships because all of us require support and encouragement to traverse our life's path.

Chapter 19

Building Resilience and Overcoming Setbacks

The process of discovering our divine mission and fulfilling it never follows a straightforward path. Everyone faces setbacks along with obstacles and deep discouragement during their life journey. Challenges that cause us pain can develop our faith as they create opportunities for personal growth. Our ability to bounce back from adversity, known as resilience, plays a vital role in handling inevitable challenges and achieving greater strength after facing them.

The development of resilience means acquiring strength from within to endure hardships, which enables learning from them before turning these experiences into growth factors. We need to develop a mindset that recognizes obstacles as chances to learn and strengthen our faith and faithfulness. This mindset shift is paramount. People need to make a purposeful shift in their outlook to perceive challenges as development opportunities instead of obstacles.

Resilience development starts with developing unshakeable faith in God's design for our existence. Active trust constitutes this belief system rather than passive belief. The conviction that God leads us through uncertain times of suffering to fulfill our destiny remains strong. This faith provides a bedrock of stability, a source of strength that sustains us through difficult times. Our difficulties serve a purpose because God has created them as components of an overarching divine strategy.

Faith often presents itself through inner assurance that we will triumph over challenges. The approach involves confronting challenges head-on with bravery because we know God accompanies us through every difficult situation. The strengthening of faith occurs through religious practices, which include prayer and meditation, along with regular scripture engagement. God leads us through our ongoing dialogue with Him to receive His wisdom while we strengthen our trust in His divine plan.

A resilient person builds their strength by establishing a solid support network. A group of positive, supportive people who provide prayer and encouragement creates a significant difference when we face challenging situations. People in our lives function as life anchors, which provide protection and support during storms, allowing us to find rest while we recharge and refocus. Relationships provide essential elements of feeling both belonged and completely loved, which help people face their setbacks.

People who provide support to us include family members and close friends and mentors, and members from our faith community. The key to success is selecting people who encourage us while holding a firm belief in our abilities and providing unconditional support through all our challenges. Sharing personal struggles while celebrating our achievements together with such individuals develops a strong sense of community bond. Such support networks enhance our determination to face obstacles while increasing our capacity for overcoming challenges.

Resilience requires self-care practices that go beyond being a comfort and must be considered essential. Our journey through life requires proper attention to physical health and emotional and spiritual well-being to handle inevitable difficulties. We need to maintain proper sleep habits while feeding our bodies wholesome foods, while doing physical activities and practicing stress relief methods, including meditation or nature time.

Emotional self-care requires us to identify and manage our feelings healthily. People find help through mental health professionals and use creativity and time with family members to cope. Spiritual self-care consists of prayer and meditation, studying the Word of God, and performing service. Self-care stands as an essential practice that allows us to develop necessary coping skills for stress management and emotional control, and balance in our lives despite facing obstacles. Our ability to bounce back from difficult situations decreases when we ignore our own care, which leaves us more susceptible to problems.

Forgiving ourselves and others represents a vital component of resilience development. Our ability to progress and embrace new opportunities becomes impossible when we keep holding onto resentment and guilt. The process of forgiveness releases anger and bitterness so we can free ourselves from past burdens, but it does not mean accepting harmful actions. The process of forgiveness may need professional guidance, but it produces transformative liberation, which enables us to face life with fresh optimism.

The act of forgiveness we give to others extends to the forgiveness we offer ourselves. We must learn to be compassionate towards our own mistakes and shortcomings, acknowledging our imperfections without defining ourselves. The fundamental element of resilience requires self-compassion because it helps people handle obstacles with empathy and understanding. We should use our failures as opportunities to learn new things instead of accepting them as proof of our worthlessness.

The development of a growth mindset plays an essential role in building resilience. A growth mindset represents the understanding that our abilities, along with our intelligence, exist to develop through our dedicated work and committed effort. Our ability to treat obstacles as growth experiences through this mindset helps us see them as development opportunities instead of signs of our inadequacy. Through this mindset, we build our capacity to stay dedicated during difficult times while using challenges to advance our growth.

Our mindset transformation requires us to change the way we talk to ourselves inside our minds. Our decision to treat challenges as chances for personal development eliminates our focus on past mistakes. The positive way we talk to ourselves acts as a source of strength that enables us to confront challenges with bravery and unwavering commitment. Positive self-talk helps people redirect their negative emotions instead of suppressing them completely.

Small victory celebrations serve as a crucial factor for both maintaining momentum and developing resilience. During our mission pursuit, we face discouraging setbacks that require us to recognize and appreciate the smallest achievements. Small victories that seem unimportant demonstrate our advancement to us. The little triumphs increase our self-assurance and solidify our confidence in reaching our targets. Positive reinforcement serves to enhance our determination because it motivates us to continue forward with optimism even during challenging times. These celebrations may be private reflections or shared moments with loved ones; the key is to acknowledge and value our progress.

Living a meaningful life requires facing multiple challenges throughout our journey. The unavoidable obstacles in life become more manageable through resilience, which enables us to handle them with poise and faith in our life's purpose. Through our dedication to God's plan and support networks and self-care practices and forgiveness work, and growth mindset development, and victory celebration, we build the necessary tools to overcome obstacles and become stronger, wiser and more connected to our divine purpose. Our journey to reach our highest potential includes encountering obstacles that make our faith stronger and our resilience more robust and reveal our purpose in life.

Chapter 20

Experiencing the Abundance of God's Blessings

Receiving God's blessings demands more than passive fortune acceptance because it requires faith-based and grateful action in life. The transition toward abundance thinking demands a different way of thinking, which moves beyond scarcity perspectives. The mentality of scarcity originates from fear, along with limited perceptions and centers on the things we do not possess. The way of thinking generates nervousness and dissatisfaction while maintaining a persistent sense of insufficiency. Abundance thinking bases its foundation on trusting God's provision while acknowledging His unlimited generosity. Our needs receive acknowledgment while we focus on the limitless wealth God provides,

which includes both physical resources and spiritual development and nurturing relationships and peaceful tranquility.

The process needs deliberate work to develop gratitude.
Gratitude exceeds basic recognition of blessings because it requires an active process to acknowledge and appreciate divine
involvement throughout every life aspect. This habit requires
daily dedication to focus on our existing possessions instead
of our absent things. Writing down three daily things we are
thankful for transforms our perspective toward blessings instead of anxieties. The practice of conscious gratitude enables
people to find abundance in all situations.

The abundant provision from God reaches further than
mere material wealth. The abundant blessings of God include
deep human relationships as well as the happiness of helping
others and the peaceful understanding that surpasses human
comprehension. We frequently dismiss these blessings when
we focus on acquiring material wealth. People seek financial
stability while ignoring the development of their relationships and the practice of kindness and spiritual growth. True
abundance brings complete well-being that includes spiritual
and emotional health and physical and relational aspects. A
life that overflows with purpose and joy and love exists.

The experience of God's abundance requires us to build
relationships with others. These relationships provide sup-

port, encouragement, and belonging. The bonds of strong relationships create a supportive network that brings comfort in difficult moments and happiness in joyful occasions. Through these relationships, we find both spiritual strength and motivation to know we do not face life's journey alone. The meaningful bonds we form in our lives serve as powerful demonstrations of God's boundless blessings.

The practice of service helps us experience more divine abundance. Through serving others, we actively demonstrate God's love and compassion to people who need assistance. The seemingly insignificant act of selflessness brings deep satisfaction and great happiness to the person performing it. The act of helping others creates an escalating chain of compassionate actions that benefits both those we assist and ourselves directly. Our service to others allows us to experience firsthand God's abundant blessings.

Through spiritual practices like prayer and meditation, we build a deeper relationship with God, which allows us to receive His abundance more deeply. Prayer serves as more than asking for material things because it represents a dialogue between believers and God while connecting heart to heart. People can express their gratitude, make confessions and seek guidance in this space. Our connection to God's will through prayer enables us to receive abundant blessings from Him.

Meditation establishes a contemplative atmosphere that enables us to develop inner awareness and discover an enduring, peaceful state that goes beyond human understanding.

Trust plays an essential role for people to experience God's abundant provision. Trust represents an active expression of faith in God's plan rather than a passive acknowledgment of current conditions when faced with difficult circumstances. We need to trust that God cares about our well-being even though we may not understand His methods. The trust we have allows us to face life's uncertainties with hope and confidence because He will provide. The belief in His sovereignty and love represents a deep trust beyond simple optimism.

The human experience naturally includes doubt and fear as inevitable elements. When doubts emerge, it becomes essential to respond with faith and trust in God's provision. You should recall all the previous times God demonstrated His loyalty to you. Read the promises in Scripture that assure you of God's provision as well as protection and guidance. Turn to your faith community for assistance while sharing your difficulties and drawing inspiration from fellow believers. During these times, prayer functions as a crucial support system that enhances your religious faith while strengthening your optimistic outlook.

The experience of God's abundance unfolds as an active process that leads us through different stages. Growth and learning, along with a stronger bond with God, define this experience. A life of patience, together with persistence and trust in God's plan, must guide us through unclear circumstances. The path of abundance leads to purpose and joy, and blessings that make the journey worthwhile despite its challenges.

We can better recognize God's abundance by understanding that every aspect of creation exists in a unified network. We exist as members of two interconnected systems, which include both our community and ecosystem. Our abundance allows us to distribute it among others, which produces a positive cycle of giving and care toward those around us. The practice of sharing reaches beyond physical goods because it includes the distribution of our time and talents and our affection. Our blessings exist for both personal enjoyment and global improvement.

The chase for abundance needs to be motivated by serving others and blessing them rather than selfish intentions. Our lives change completely when we understand abundance through this specific perspective. Our mindset transitions from individual achievement to becoming agents of positive change for the world. A life of true purpose emerges when we see things from this perspective because it fulfills God's plan for us. We become vessels of blessings to spread God's love and generosity to everyone we meet, beyond the reception of divine blessings.

The experience of God's abundance exists beyond perfect living. A person should dedicate themselves to faith, together with trust and gratitude for their life. Life will occasionally present us with periods of uncertainty and feelings of being overwhelmed, and doubts about our beliefs. Despite all circumstances, God's love, along with His grace, remains constant. God remains present in all situations while continuously guiding to lead us toward abundant living. You should begin the journey with an open heart while trusting His provision and believing in His boundless blessings for those who seek Him. Faith-based living means living a life that overflows with blessings from God. We have been summoned to establish a legacy that combines faith with hope and unwavering trust in God's benevolence.

Chapter 21

Life with Meaning: The Impact

The lasting impact we create surpasses physical objects because it represents how we touch the hearts and minds of others, while our decisions make waves across time. When we follow God's call, our legacy transforms into a powerful and significant force. Through faith and selfless service, we establish a powerful legacy that demonstrates the transformative effect of these qualities. This legacy acts as a source of motivation that both strengthens others and creates positive global transformations.

The life God called us to live extends past grand achievements because it appears through ordinary choices which demonstrate our spiritual values and Godly purpose. The power of positive energy spreads through our world because of simple acts like giving kindness and listening to friends in need, and praying silently for strangers' well-being. These everyday actions generate ripples that transform lives in ways that we cannot always see.

A teacher who teaches students to love learning creates an enduring impact on their students' lives by developing their minds while guiding their future paths. Through their classroom work, this teacher builds a legacy that produces numerous future students who later transform their communities by acting as change-makers. Parents who teach their children moral values create adults who become positive forces in society by using their faith-based character traits to help others. Through their actions and choices, the children will create a lasting impact on the world. A parent's religious dedication to their children creates a continuous expansion of positive influence that continues across multiple generations.

A meaningful life achieves increased impact because of mentorship. Through our dedication to helping others, we teach them how to find their life purpose by sharing our expertise and faith knowledge. Through mentoring others, we enable them to experience meaningful lives. The process of mentoring younger individuals gives both parties life enrichment while creating within the mentor a sense of accomplishment from developing the next generation. The continuous process of mentorship and discipleship creates an endless chain of beneficial impacts that extends our legacy into future eras.

Our lasting impact emerges from both our life accomplishments together with the connections we form with others. The meaningful relationships we build with our family, friends and community enhance our existence while creating enduring bonds that transcend our physical existence. Through these relationships, we obtain assistance together with support and develop feelings of belonging. These relationships enhance our quality of life while building a lasting legacy of affection that remains after we pass away. The legacy we create consists of the indistinct yet powerful elements, which include our relationships and shared memories, as well as our expressions of love. Strong, loving relationships build better communities, which make future generations more resilient and devoted to their faith.

A meaningful existence requires handling challenges while enduring difficult times. Although these obstacles prove challenging, they create opportunities for personal development as well as building resilience. Through trials, our character becomes exposed, and our faith is tested, which makes us stronger in our purpose. The wisdom we acquire through experience, together with the lessons learned through hardship and our ability to persevere, builds a richer and more meaningful legacy. These obstacles can transform into remarkable tales of faith and endurance, which motivate people to defeat their own challenges.

A person achieves meaningful existence by consistently striving to achieve faith and excellence while serving others. The path to living a meaningful life involves maintaining consistent action alignment with our beliefs and practicing our values across all parts of our existence. The path toward meaningful living brings challenges, yet it brings rewards in both this life and the next that cannot be measured. Our legacy emerges from our accomplishments and demonstrates our absolute dedication to God's divine mission.

A legacy that matters develops through embracing forgiveness. The practice of holding onto bitterness and resentment causes damage to ourselves because it prevents us from experiencing peace and joy in life. Forgiveness toward ourselves and others enables us to advance toward positive possibilities by releasing ourselves from negative bonds. Through forgiveness, we establish a healing legacy that spreads restoration to everyone we touch and extends across multiple generations.

A legacy that matters develops through ongoing growth since our lives become a continuous path of development and change. The path to reach our goal is what matters rather than reaching the goal itself. Our dedication exists in creating a life that fulfills God's intended purpose for us.

Use the challenges to celebrate victories while following God's guidance to create a legacy that will extend past your death. Through living according to God's plan, your life transforms into a hopeful source of inspiration that demonstrates faith's power for future generations. The everlasting legacy of a meaningful life provides both a world benefit and spiritual evidence, along with a meaningful inheritance.

Chapter 22

Sharing Your Gifts with Others

A purposeful life reaches its peak when we create meaningful effects on the lives of others. God gives us special talents that we need to distribute freely across the world. The process of sharing creates a vital element for developing an everlasting legacy that extends beyond our earthly existence. We must identify ourselves as tools of divine grace because our abilities serve to motivate others while boosting their strength and inspiring them.

Our gifts find an excellent platform to be shared through different mentorship approaches. We should direct others by teaching valuable lessons while showing them their personal destiny. This process creates equal or greater benefits for mentors compared to mentees. The process of sharing wisdom leads to a better awareness of personal talents and challenges. The process leads to growth at both individual and spiritual levels. Such experiences deepen our religious ties and reveal God's divine plan to us.

When an experienced artist mentors a novice apprentice, they show patience in teaching them their artistic skills. When we teach others, we transfer essential abilities and develop a dedication to perfection that brings meaning and satisfaction to the students. The mentor both enhances their expertise and develops their skills through sharing, and gives the apprentice something more valuable than technical training, which includes the spiritual faith that drives the mentor's work. The apprentice's potential to become a mentor will create a continuous chain of inspirational development across numerous generations.

The practice of mentorship reaches beyond creative fields. A veteran business expert should guide emerging entrepreneurs through their startup journey while teaching them ethical business principles and strong work ethic values. Mentorship provides essential knowledge while simultaneously teaching faith-based business principles. The mentorship relationship will generate benefits that will reach future generations. The influence of faith-based mentorship enables people to make the world better for those around them. The mentoring role of a faith-based teacher serves the community through spiritual leadership in an environment where faith-based education is scarce. The faith-based mentoring relationship between parent and child produces an enormous influence that extends across many generations ahead.

The practice of gift-sharing does not need formal mentorship structures. The act of offering an attentive ear to someone in need, along with encouraging during difficult times, serves as a simple way to share gifts. The use of our talents through local charity work creates positive change in our community. The practice of sharing our faith includes showing compassion and kindness through understanding actions. These small service actions, which seem unimportant on their own, form into a strong positive force that transforms people and builds an everlasting legacy.

Through teaching, we share our gifts in their most expansive interpretation. The process of knowledge transmission helps people develop curiosity and establish learning love in others. A teacher who inspires his students to love learning will create a lasting effect that reaches well after their educational years. The educational impact creates learners who transform into change agents throughout their communities and the wider world. Students learn faith values in addition to secular teachings to develop into professionals and social members who practice their faith.

Teaching does not need a classroom setting because it can emerge through different teaching methods. The act of sharing our expertise with others through workshops and tutorials, and meaningful conversations produces remarkable effects. Our faith needs to integrate with our skill-sharing process while we also share God's wisdom and grace. Our legacy is to influence future generations through this approach.

A lasting legacy requires the inspiration of upcoming generations to achieve meaningful change. We should start by giving hope to others while nurturing dreams and enabling them to follow their passions. Our mission includes mentorship of young people and storytelling about faith and perseverance, and living a lifestyle that represents the values we want to pass down. Our actions, together with words, create long-lasting effects that affect future generations in their choices and actions.

A parent who teaches their children about strong moral values creates a lasting effect on their descendants. To achieve this goal, we teach children about faith and compassion alongside service towards others. These children will grow up to become parents who will continue the legacy of faith and service that they learned from their parents. The extensive chain reaction affects people across multiple generations within both families and communities. The faith-based teachings and mentoring that children receive will expand exponentially to transform their world.

Through our professional work, we possess the ability to inspire upcoming generations. Through their dedication to healing the sick and inspiring others through their artistry, physicians and artists created enduring impacts that influenced numerous people while motivating future generations to serve others. Our faith-based work principles create positive effects that benefit our entire community.

Our gifts become an expression of faith because they represent the divine purpose that exists within our lives. We must accept our special talents to serve God and benefit others. The sharing of our abilities provides us with a sacred opportunity to transform the world and establish a meaningful legacy that will benefit generations to come through our faith-based actions.

Our constructed legacy serves as both a divine expression of our faith commitment and a human benefit. Our words, together with our actions, create a worldwide impact that extends beyond our current existence. A legacy that endures represents the authentic significance of lasting heritage. A life dedicated to God's plan produces a lasting impact that remains strong through time.

Chapter 23

Making a Difference in Your Community

Our influence surpasses our individual surroundings because it penetrates into the areas where we live. Our accomplishments as individuals have built our legacy together with our dedication to serving the well-being of our local community. Our community involvement goes beyond charity because it represents an essential aspect of fulfilling God's purpose for us. Through this opportunity, we have the chance to help God's mission by using our hands and feet to spread love across the world. A single act of kindness performed in a community creates a chain reaction of compassion that reshapes human experiences in the world.

Several paths exist to make contributions. Three examples of volunteer work include helping at soup kitchens and visiting older people in nursing homes, and mentoring youth who are at risk. These actions represent genuine faith expressions that show God's love concretely operating through us. The service activity produces blessings between people that go beyond mere self-giving because it involves the exchange of blessings. We find abundance through selfless giving because we gain a deeper religious connection, develop a stronger life purpose, and gain deeper knowledge about the human condition.

The effects of volunteering create results that extend further than what we immediately see. Such service helps create stronger community relationships while building partnerships and establishing common objectives.

Our professional abilities possess great potential to support community development. The medical profession uses doctors to provide clinic care, while lawyers offer free legal services to those who need them, and architects build structures through their work. Three examples demonstrate how our specialized knowledge can transform into service for the community. Our professional actions express both our faith-based commitment to serving society and our capability as experts. Our skill application enhances the quality and integrity of services by demonstrating values that align with our faith. Through this approach, we establish a powerful demonstration that extends beyond professional settings to affect all our community relationships.

Being present among our neighbors produces substantial effects on our communities. When we listen to their issues while offering motivational words and extending help, our community develops stronger ties, and members feel a sense of community. People who feel isolated or marginalized experience deep changes because of these minimal yet significant actions. Human connection stands as the basic building block to develop community structures and build faith through caring and compassionate actions.

Service opportunities are boundless. People can impact their communities by planning community cleanup events while leading Bible study groups and building mentorship programs for youth. Such initiatives demand dedication and work but provide countless benefits to participants. These programs lead to concrete community enhancements and both spiritual development and enduring relationships. By starting such initiatives, we demonstrate our faith-based leadership while motivating others to help create a service-oriented community.

The impact of faith-based organizations on community development remains transformative. Churches, along with other faith-based institutions, maintain critical services, which include food banks and homeless shelters, and educational programs. These organizations maintain their position as fundamental community support structures because they create safety networks for vulnerable populations while building resilience. Faith organizations enrich the community with spiritual guidance, moral support, and belonging. The active expression of faith through service constitutes a practical example of love and care, which results in community transformation. Beyond formal organizations, faith-based initiatives can make a difference. These three examples include organizing a neighborhood watch program to improve safety, starting a book club to promote intellectual development, and creating a community garden to advance healthy living. The initiatives unite different groups of people who develop opportunities for interaction and generate a stronger community life. These initiatives draw their roots from our faith principles to show practical care for the common good.

We should establish a community legacy through continuous selfless work instead of seeking major accomplishments. The development of empathy and understanding, along with mutual support, forms the core of this process. Building relationships requires trust, along with respect and shared commitment to serve the common good. A legacy built by such actions will last longer than our lifetime and motivate upcoming generations to maintain and improve the service work that we established.

Community service functions as an effective expression of our religious faith. Our beliefs manifest in real-world actions, which show God's love through compassionate and kind deeds. Our consistent dedication to community service proves the transformative nature of faith beyond any spoken words. The external display of our faith develops an ongoing relationship that strengthens our faith and creates a continuous cycle between faith and action.

We establish a meaningful legacy through the positive influence we bring to people's lives and our communities, along with the world at large. Every person should discover their individual abilities to use for God's service and to help others. The objective of making a positive change in others' lives stands above all personal goals. Through this process, our lives become more purposeful and joyful. Through our tangible faith activities in communities, we create a chain reaction that reaches future populations while reshaping the world permanently. The true sign of living a meaningful existence. This existence produces a lasting impact through faith-based service, which fosters human development. This ultimate legacy expresses the divine mission that exists within all human beings. Our most important gift to the world consists of the legacy built by faith and action, which will stand as our most enduring monument.

Chapter 24

Inspiring Others to Find Their Calling

The purposeful life we lead transforms us into motivational guides who lead people toward discovering their life direction. We serve as guidance lights for others after discovering God's intended destiny for ourselves. To inspire others, we need to create conditions that motivate them to discover their God-given talents and hidden passions.

Consider mentorship's profound impact. Our personal life experiences, including our achievements and our mistakes, serve as valuable guidance to those searching for direction. Through our life stories, which incorporate faith and resilience, we create motivational instruments that help others. These experiences demonstrate that finding your purpose requires facing obstacles yet leads to satisfying outcomes. Our role as mentors involves helping others uncover their individual life paths by giving them support during their discovery. Sharing our personal battles creates a sense of solidarity for others who experience similar obstacles when they seek to fulfill their life purpose. When we share our weaknesses alongside our faith in God's plan, we build genuine relationships that foster profound personal development.

The practice of paying attention actively results in a deep transformation of others. Many people face difficulties when trying to express their personal ambitions because they battle with internal doubts and outside pressures. To help them speak freely about their ideas and emotions, we must create an environment of complete support and non-judgment. Trustful listening enables people to discover their inner world while remaining sheltered from criticism. The practice of attentive listening builds stronger connections between mentors and mentees while deepening their self-knowledge. Through active listening, people gain time to reflect on their ideas and emotions, which helps them identify their special life path.

The way we conduct ourselves inspires other people in addition to our mentoring roles. Our purposeful existence serves as evidence to show the potential of following God's guidance. Our dedication to following our divine purpose shows others that pursuing one's passions leads to complete happiness and meaningful service. When we use our faith and talents, and gifts to follow God's purpose, it creates a living demonstration that becomes a gentle inspiration for others to do the same. Our intentional life actions convey a sermon that surpasses the power of spoken words.

To help others find their purpose, we should help them break free from their restrictive mental barriers. People fail to advance because they doubt themselves and fear failure while facing expectations from their social environment. We should approach these beliefs with care to help people understand their natural value and special abilities. When encouraging someone, we should use biblical passages together with contemplation exercises about their personal strengths. Through God's power, people can transcend seemingly unbreakable obstacles. Helping people understand their own value and talents will enable them to embrace God's mission for their lives.

Exploring passionate pursuits stands as an essential requirement for helping people discover their purpose. People can explore their interests through volunteer opportunities in fields that match their personal passions. The process of supporting their educational development or training process should also be encouraged. They require basic tools and backing, which enable them to advance to the following step.

The support we give others reveals their inner strength so they can achieve maximum potential and fulfill their purpose. The assistance we provide will move them toward discovering their God-given abilities.

The development of a reflective framework holds equal importance. Individuals who practice quiet contemplation or encouraged prayer can find their way to inner awareness to identify their special gifts and life mission. These practices serve more than self-analysis purposes because they help people develop spiritually while deepening their bond with God. The process helps people recognize their individual abilities together with their purpose while connecting it to God's divine plan. The practice of leading others through spiritual exercises leads to a more significant spiritual experience for them. These practices allow people to receive numerous blessings and opportunities that God has in store. The process of inspiring people to find their meaning requires both patience and empathy alongside unwavering faith. We occasionally need to guide people away from their comfort boundaries to show them that personal development emerges when confronting obstacles. The journey toward spiritual growth depends on their support since it helps them develop faith in God's plan. Different forms of support exist to help others achieve their goals, yet receiving help from others plays a vital role.

The discovery of purpose through inspiration leads others to find their purpose, which exceeds any measure. People who discover their life purpose and live according to their values transform into forces that generate positive change throughout the world. The individual contributions may seem insignificant, yet they merge together to enrich the lives of people outside their individual scope. Empowering others to achieve their complete potential leads to a world where compassion and creative service flourish. Each person discovers their purpose while successfully influencing those around them through the positive influence they create. The positive feedback mechanism creates a perpetual cycle that transforms and motivates numerous people.

Our connection to our purpose develops when we motivate others to identify their life mission. Our dedication to a purposeful existence becomes stronger when we dedicate ourselves to helping others achieve their life goals. When we share our experiences with others while guiding them on their paths, we experience deep personal transformation that brings back our life purpose. The experience of outreach leads to a deepened connection with God that enhances our faith while strengthening our commitment. Our relationship with

God and His plan receives additional rewards because of this rewarding process.

A teacher serves as an example by motivating a student to study medicine. The mentor helps a young entrepreneur launch their business while the parents support their child to develop their artistic abilities. These little encouragement actions produce remarkable effects that guide people toward their future and enhance the world for everyone. Such ordinary gestures produce enduring, transformative effects that impact both people's personal growth and global development. These basic actions form the foundation for creating a world based on hope and compassion. Our inspirational efforts reach beyond our immediate surroundings to establish a heritage that spans across multiple generations. Our efforts to help others discover their purpose create a worldwide impact of meaningful lives and fulfillment for countless people. The continuous chain of inspiration will enhance our religious beliefs while deepening our knowledge about God's master plan. This legacy exists as a combination of faith-based empowerment alongside hope. This profound heritage will influence our existence throughout multiple years ahead.

Inspiring others to discover their purpose represents the core element for creating a meaningful legacy that truly matters. The act of reaching others through our influence reaches farther than our individual lifetime. Through mentoring and guiding others toward their God-given potential, we help create a world where people live in alignment with their divine destiny. Through this approach, we establish a society that is filled with happiness and faith leads to transformation. The world will receive our ultimate contribution through the establishment of a legacy that brings hope and inspiration that will persist across numerous generations. This legacy represents the most impactful change we can make on the world that surrounds us.

Chapter 25

Creating a Lasting Impact Beyond Your Lifetime

Our purpose extends further than our life expectancy because we create enduring effects that will survive beyond our death. Our intentional life creates eternal effects that transcend human years. Our actions, together with our choices and our unshakeable dedication to our divinely given purpose, create waves that extend far past our physical death. A true inheritance surpasses physical possessions because it enables faith-based legacies that will encourage future generations. This practice establishes a spiritual inheritance that demonstrates how a life following God's plans can transform people. One major way to establish enduring impact involves mentoring and discipling others. Through investing time with others to help them identify their divine purpose, we build an enduring impact that exceeds our lifetime. The purpose of mentoring others is to help them find their authentic potential rather than to manipulate their actions. We provide guidance to empower people to discover their authentic abilities and find meaning in their lives. Through mentor guidance, people develop life-altering experiences that motivate upcoming generations. Our stories containing achievements along with setbacks function as essential resources for people who want to establish their own paths. Our authentic disclosure of weaknesses creates empowerment for others by demonstrating they share common struggles, while God provides enough strength for all obstacles.

Through active participation in Kingdom work, we establish our legacy. The Kingdom work extends beyond formal religious responsibilities into all domains of life. We make substantial contributions to our community through both community service activities and by being people of integrity and compassion. These actions aren't just acts of service.

Our faith-based actions represent both the physical manifestation of our devotion to God's mission and the permanent foundation for future success. Our help of others in any way produces effects that extend beyond our life expectancy.

A lasting legacy requires us to establish something that continues to exist after our physical death. People can leave their legacy through writing inspirational books or creating music that moves others and making art that touches hearts. The establishment of charitable organizations and foundations by founders leads to sustained community service after their death. The establishment of lasting works that inspire and uplift people while promoting faith, compassion, and service, remains as eternal evidence of our life's work. These creations express our commitment to our faith and values.

Establishing a permanent legacy demands both purposeful action and deliberate effort from us. The process demands both introspection and prayer and a dedication to follow the path which God has designated for our lives. Our pursuit of God's guidance needs to be continuous as we remain open to His direction while trusting His divine plan for our existence. This spiritual path demonstrates our religious conviction regarding God's authority and His destiny for human existence. Continuous spiritual development becomes possible through our dedication to becoming like Jesus while expressing His divine love and compassion.

We create enduring legacies through building meaningful relationships with others. The bonds we establish with family members and friends, along with colleagues and community members, integrate into our permanent effects. Our relationships bring depth to our existence through their supportive nature and motivational strength, and sense of belonging. The connections we establish function as channels to distribute our influence while creating enduring bonds of affection and relationships. The relationships that we establish today will continue to exist after our death to create networks of support that help those we care about. Our positive influence reaches beyond death to shape the future of upcoming generations.

A permanent legacy exists beyond wealth and recognition because it means enhancing the state of the world. The pursuit of a lasting legacy involves leading an existence based on moral principles and kindness while making meaningful impacts on others. When we reflect on God's love and grace in our lives, we create an inspiring example for others to follow His path. Our most valuable contribution to the world derives from our acts of giving rather than from our accumulated possessions. Our giving back serves as evidence of both our religious devotion and our dedication to fulfill God's divine plan.

A person's lasting legacy mirrors the way they choose to live their life. This legacy serves as proof of our faith, together with our core beliefs and our dedication to our divine purpose. Our legacy extends beyond death when we dedicate our lives to God's will while investing in others and making positive changes in our community. The lasting legacy proves our devotion to God and demonstrates the power of living a life dedicated to His glory. Through faith and hope and love, we build a legacy that will motivate future generations. The eternal legacy we built demonstrates God's divine grace while showcasing our absolute dedication to His divine plan. Our legacy will continue to inspire and uplift future generations for many centuries ahead. Our eternal legacy stands as a world gift that embodies our absolute dedication to our unshakeable faith.

Chapter 26

Reaffirming Your Calling

R eaffirming your calling requires ongoing faith practice rather than being a single moment of commitment. You must renew your sacred vows to your life's creator every day. The practice of choosing your purpose remains an intentional decision that stands above the noise of everyday life and responsibilities. This dedication serves to unite your heart and mind with your actions to fulfill the divine purpose that shapes your existence.

Perform quiet introspection to analyze your behaviors while evaluating their connection to your life purpose. Evaluate each decision you make daily to verify its alignment with your divine assignment. Am I using my resources to back activities that help fulfill my divine life purpose? If not, what adjustments need to be made? The process of honest self-examination remains essential to maintain faithfulness to your life path.

Your commitment needs to be reaffirmed through prayer, which serves as an essential tool. Devote yourself to prayer with God to receive His guidance and receive His strength. Present your doubts and fears and uncertainties to Him so He can give you peace and reassurance. The true nature of prayer involves sacred communication with God, which deepens your bond with the power that gives your life its purpose. When you pray in silence, God's voice will have the power to enter your spiritual nature. Pay close attention to the gentle hints that the Holy Spirit provides through subtle confirmation signals and soft whispers.

The path to success requires someone to be accountable to you. Tell your commitment to people you trust, including friends and family members and mentors who can give you support and encouragement and create a secure environment for openness. The shared journey creates a sense of community while offering different perspectives that might otherwise go unnoticed. A supportive network serves as your accountability system to help you maintain dedication to your purpose. You should pick people to confide in your most personal matters who will help you rise rather than criticize you.

Make a point to celebrate all your successes, regardless of their size. Recognize all the achievements you have accomplished and every barrier you have successfully passed. The power of gratitude helps restore your spirit and leads to greater accomplishments. The purpose of these celebrations is to honor God's active role in your life journey through acknowledging His guidance and expressing gratitude for blessings. Acknowledge the divine grace that has enabled you to reach these moments.

You should welcome every failure and mistake because they offer chances to develop further. Such moments are natural components of your life path, which deliver important educational experiences that strengthen your comprehension of your life purpose. Rather than viewing setbacks as defeats, consider them detours on the path. Through this experience, you will gain knowledge while improving your flexibility and increasing your dedication. Such challenges make apparent the hidden abilities that exist within you as well as the surprising opportunities for development.

You should consistently work to develop your knowledge and skills, which support your life mission. You can improve your abilities and deepen your understanding through resources including books, workshops, mentorships and educational programs. The continuous pursuit of knowledge remains vital to maintain your position of influence and maintain your dedication to your life purpose. Remain both curious and open to fresh knowledge and fresh viewpoints.

Your commitment develops over time through experiences while remaining dynamic in its nature. Your journey toward purpose will become more profound as your methods become more refined and your actions evolve through the process of growth and maturity. Your connection to the divine becomes more evident through this continuous process of growth. Success demands that you welcome change together with flexibility.

Cultivate a spirit of generosity and service. You should discover methods to use your skills and abilities to make positive impacts on others while pursuing your life's meaning. When you dedicate yourself to serving others, your own life will become richer, and you will discover increased purpose. Giving back serves as a fundamental element in living a life that aligns with divine will because it establishes feelings of unity and meaningful contributions.

Practice self-compassion. Living a life devoted to divine meaning requires effort because this journey does not come without difficulty. You will encounter moments of self-doubt, together with feelings of disappointment and hopelessness. When self-doubt arises, show yourself compassion. Acknowledge your struggles while looking for support from others or through prayer.

You need to spend time with a group of people who have similar interests. Seek individuals who both understand your life path and support you while having the same desire to fulfill your divine purpose. The supportive network gives members both encouragement as well as accountability and creates a sense of belonging. The community helps with personal development and enhances resistance.

Your dedication to your life purpose demonstrates your religious beliefs. Your dedication to living according to a divine life plan stands as evidence of your religious beliefs. Your divine value gets recognized through this commitment to lead a purposeful existence. Your absolute dedication will change your life, yet it will create effects on others that might exceed your understanding. Although the path to living your divine purpose may stretch over time, it will lead you to a life of unmatched fulfillment. Your existence becomes meaningful and creates lasting changes while filling you with eternal happiness. Trust in the process and trust in the divine plan that is unfolding throughout your life.

Chapter 27

Embracing the Ongoing Journey of My Faith

L ife purpose alignment requires lifelong growth with continuous discovery and unshakable faith. The fundamental ongoing nature of spiritual development enables us to handle unavoidable difficulties and welcome success throughout our journey. The process evolves as we mature and acquire knowledge, which deepens our spiritual connection with ourselves and the Divine. The summit at the mountain peak represents the complete achievement of your life purpose. The real character development, together with essential life lessons, occurs during the mountain ascent, which features diverse landscapes and unpredictable weather conditions.

The main element of this everlasting spiritual quest involves ongoing self-identification. Our comprehension of God-given talents and passions will evolve and become more refined when we move forward. Our deep beliefs from five years ago now seem less important today, and this natural change is completely acceptable and expected. The natural evolution of our spiritual path serves as proof of spiritual development and God's purposeful transformation of our destiny. As humans, we exist beyond being unchanging objects because our lives change continuously because of experiences and God's blessings and our relationships.

A flexible approach, along with adaptation, becomes necessary for accepting fluidity in life. The initial view of our life purpose needs periodic modifications as well as readjustments, and complete reconsiderations because of new insights and unanticipated life events. The changing direction reflects our improving comprehension of our life path rather than indicating a lack of guidance. As you navigate through the stars, remember that the constellations stay unchanged, but your position changes as you journey. Our course needs constant recalculation to match our moving position as life's changing winds affect us.

This ongoing journey requires sustained learning as one of its essential pillars. Our divine assignment usually unfolds through time by adding layers of understanding, which we uncover through deliberate learning activities. The journey of purposeful exploration reveals both unanticipated abilities and novel opportunities and forces us to develop our competencies despite unexpected barriers. Our continuous development alongside the adaptation process keeps us actively involved in our life purpose while maintaining both excitement and relevance to our mission.

Learning beyond basic knowledge acquisition demands an insatiable curiosity that maintains our growth and keeps us engaged with the changing world. People learn in various ways, including formal education and workshops and seminars and mentorship and relevant literature study and meaningful dialogues with like-minded individuals. These educational approaches enable students to achieve different levels of learning advancement. Our main priority should be to accept diverse viewpoints and recognize challenges as learning experiences while actively developing our knowledge base and abilities.

The continuous journey depends on prayer as our main support system. The practice of prayer goes beyond set words because it develops into an active dialogue between humans and God. We use this time to examine ourselves and seek guidance while showing appreciation to God and surrendering our will to His direction. Through prayer, we gain better insight into our life's purpose. During difficult times, we receive power from God while experiencing comfort because of His unchanging divine presence.

Consider contemplative prayer. This is a time for quiet reflection. Through contemplative prayer, we let God's spirit flow through us while listening for the soft messages of the Holy Spirit. This practice enables us to find God's gentle inner guidance that leads us on our life path.

The importance of community cannot be overstated. The essential element for maintaining motivation and dealing with obstacles in our divine purpose journey is to surround ourselves with like-minded people who encourage and support each other's mission. These individuals hold us accountable while questioning our views and deliver essential help when we doubt or feel despair. When we share our journey with others, we experience belonging, which creates supportive networks to maintain our dedication. Our community functions as a secure environment where we can openly discuss our challenges while celebrating our achievements. To find such a community, one can search within faith-based organizations or support groups or establish mentoring relationships or simply connect with friends pursuing similar goals. A setback serves as a valuable moment for personal advancement. The path of challenges, together with disappointments, does not equal failure because they help us develop a stronger understanding and build resilience. These experiences develop our comprehension of our purpose in life. These moments point out specific areas that require improvement while showing talents we were unaware we had. Through challenges, we gain patience as well as humility and perseverance. Through faith, we gain the ability to see God's divine intervention in our difficulties. Our total personal development benefits from every experience we encounter. The experiences we face enable us to build a stronger faith that becomes more resilient.

Our advancement depends on recognizing and celebrating every triumph, regardless of its size. When we recognize God's role in our achievements, we can stay humble and grateful while avoiding becoming proud or complacent. Our commitment to our purpose strengthens through victory celebrations, which also show us the advancement we have achieved. This drives us to pursue our objectives with greater determination. People celebrate their victories through both personal contemplation and group events with their loved ones. These events serve to both convey personal achievements and express gratitude for received blessings.

Your dedication to your purpose serves as a test of your faith. Your commitment serves as proof of your belief in the divine plan. Your commitment demonstrates understanding of your natural value while dedicating yourself to creating meaningful purpose in life. Your unwavering dedication will change your life while producing effects that extend far beyond your understanding. The long and winding path leads to a destination that is a life completely in sync with divine purpose. The life you experience will be deep in meaning while creating enduring effects and yielding enduring joy. Trust in the process, and above all, trust in the Divine plan unfolding in your life. It's a journey of faith. The nature of faith requires continuous development, which leads us to grow deeper in our trust in God's eternal love and divine guidance.

Chapter 28

Celebrating God's Grace and Provision

We must honor the grace and provision of God as they form the fundamental foundation that directs our path toward divine purpose. The earth provides an ideal environment where our natural abilities and interests grow to maturity. God's guidance remains constant to navigate turbulent waters, and He provides continuous support during our moments of weakness. Our mission to find purpose will lack humility and gratitude if we do not deeply value God's unlimited blessings.

The journey to fulfill God's divine plan requires spiritual awareness as its essential foundation. The core definition of spirituality involves becoming aware of and responding to God's active presence in our daily existence. Our spiritual practice demands an intentional search for God's involvement in every facet of our existence, starting from tiny everyday occurrences all the way to major life achievements. We should develop a thankful heart that produces abundant gratitude for His ongoing provision and care.

Every day, we experience miracles that we fail to recognize because we ignore the sun's heat on our bodies, the lovely sunrise, the playful sounds of children, and the loving bonds with our family and friends. The small blessings we experience in our daily lives represent physical expressions of God's love and his continuous watchful presence in our world. Through gratitude, we develop greater sensitivity toward the abundant wealth that exists everywhere. We start to detect the divine presence in every situation, from significant events to tiny moments of spiritual guidance and reassurance.

Consider all the hurdles you conquered, along with every hurdle you jumped beyond your limits and all the challenges you successfully handled. God's divine grace and provision become evident through each of these accomplishments. During times of hardship, it becomes natural to focus on our problems, yet we should instead look for God's leadership through the challenges. Our view transforms when we look at life to show God directing us through tough times while

His power upholds us and His love completely surrounds us. Life's difficulties create spaces for personal development, which leads to stronger faith and a clearer understanding of God's purpose.

God bestows talents and passions upon each person as specific gifts which He designed with precision to fulfill their life mission. Recognizing and celebrating these gifts represents an act of worship because it shows appreciation for the divine artistry that shapes our existence. These gifts are not.

The divine plan includes giving these gifts to share them with others to create beneficial changes throughout the world. The more we use our gifts, the more they grow, and our knowledge of purpose deepens, and we feel happy while serving others. The act of using our gifts becomes a thankful expression to the God who gives all good gifts.

God provides us with abundant blessings that reach beyond material possessions to envelop our emotional lives, our spiritual connection and our relationships with others. God's abundant provision reaches further than our physical requirements because it includes both direction and power as well as reassurance and tranquility. During times of hardship, God provides the power to stay strong, along with wisdom to find direction and peace to heal. When we lose our direction, He guides us through the challenges we face. When we experience negative environments, He gives us peace and hope. Our ability to recognize and value God's abundant provision will strengthen our capacity to defeat challenges while we confidently work toward our life purpose.

God's provision deserves both personal and group acknowledgment in the act of celebration. Our faith grows stronger when we reveal our experiences of divine grace to others while inspiring them and creating community bonds. When we share our life stories about God's intervention, we both recognize His work in our lives while offering hope to people who encounter similar hardships. The act of sharing testimonies creates a united community that provides a supportive space for members to celebrate their triumphs and find solace during difficult times.

Fostering a spirit of gratitude and celebration means more than simply feeling thankful because it develops an intense God-centered bond through which we understand His complete control in our existence and follow His guidance. The process of recognizing abundant grace and provision continues throughout our lives because it requires a lifelong commitment.

Our spiritual journey exists within community since we travel together with believers who experience both the challenges and victories of living according to divine purpose.

Through shared experiences of success and mutual support during challenges, we create a unified force that makes our faith stronger and enables us to continue forward. This supportive atmosphere allows members to share their doubts and insecurities together with their triumphs without fear of judgment. The environment welcomes our vulnerabilities and delivers encouragement without restraint.

God's grace and provision stand as an essential component rather than an optional addition to our search for life's purpose. Our lives are constructed upon this foundation, which provides direction through its compass and maintains our forward motion. A heart of gratitude combined with God's life-wide presence and story-sharing about His grace will guide us toward meaningful experiences and lasting fulfillment, and enduring happiness. The journey will guide us toward achieving complete alignment with our divine destiny. Our existence exists as a thankful response to the endless love and provision from our Creator. Our life's journey manifests as evidence of God's grace while demonstrating our faith and serving as motivation for others. The path continues to reveal discoveries while our faith deepens, and we strengthen our trust in God's divine plan. Open your heart to this journey while maintaining complete faith in the divine plan that unfolds in your life. God's grace will reshape your existence while extending its blessings to those who surround you.

Chapter 29

Looking Towards the Future with Hope and Expectation

Moving forward into the future requires us to maintain both steadfast hope and faithful anticipation after understanding our divine mission and God's plan for our lives. This stance is not a form of idle dreaming but a mindful way of maintaining mental focus. We know this because God exists as a loving sovereign being who controls every detail of our existence. Our path of self-discovery led us to discover our true value as well as the special gifts and abilities God gave us. We have faced our doubts and confronted our fears while celebrating all the big and small victories that occurred during our journey.

The path before us remains unclear at certain moments when we face the future. Life contains hidden surprises and unanticipated challenges, together with unanticipated chances. Our faith takes its most prominent position during this period. God's eternal plan stands as the most essential trust for us during times of uncertainty. The Lord reveals his plans for you in Jeremiah 29:11 by saying, "plans to prosper you and not harm you, plans to give you hope and a future." This scripture presents an active summons to welcome the future with assurance rather than passive, idle dreaming.

Our expectation stems from a deep comprehension of God's nature rather than empty positive thinking. This belief derives from our understanding of His character as a faithful God who upholds His vows and sees beyond the present moment to guide all things toward good outcomes for His loving people (Romans 8:28). The storms of life do not prevent God from actively guiding us toward the achievement of His divine plan.

A constant relationship with God through prayer helps to develop our trust in Him. Prayer functions beyond asking for things because it establishes a dialogical connection with God. The prayer space allows us to reveal our innermost thoughts while expressing our concerns and receiving guidance from God, together with comfort. Through prayer, we develop inner strength and gain both clarity and fresh hope. Through prayer, we develop the ability to hear His voice above worldly distractions so we can get the wisdom and guidance we need to travel through upcoming challenges.

To embrace the future with hope, people must establish a faith-based community. When we place ourselves among believers who understand our experience and provide support, it creates powerful supportive bonds. The community provides us with both safety during difficult times and joy when we experience successes. When we share our life stories, including our difficulties and successes with others, our faith becomes stronger while inspiring others to do the same. Our sense of belonging grows through this practice, which shows us we are never truly alone during our life journey.

God has already written the design of the future into existence. We may not observe the complete picture, but we can trust the artist's ability and artistic vision. We must add our distinctive abilities, along with our faith and passions, to the work that God is developing. Our task involves taking an active role in His plan by showing faith through the pursuit of opportunities while keeping our hearts open to His direction.

Actively pursuing service opportunities represents an important aspect of embracing a hopeful future. Our natural abilities, along with our life passions, exist to be shared with others because they serve as divine gifts for positive impact in the world. Our gifts used for serving others allow us to accomplish our life purpose and discover happiness and purpose through the positive impact we create for others. Through this service, we demonstrate our gratitude to God's grace and provision while physically showing our faith and love for Him.

The path ahead will present both obstacles and chances for success. During this time, our faith receives its tests as well as its refinements. Setbacks exist as stepping stones toward growth because they offer chances for personal development and learning alongside character strengthening. These situations present us with opportunities to strengthen our divine bond while drawing more deeply on His power to become more resilient.

The path to fulfill God's purpose in our lives extends beyond a specific point because it develops through ongoing spiritual growth. We need to dedicate our entire lifetime to discovering His intentions and executing His instructions while following His teachings. Each day offers fresh opportunities to discover our purpose while utilizing our gifts to experience happiness from living according to God's divine plan.

Our upcoming destiny exists beyond what happened in our past and what we experience today because it depends on our faith commitment to God's plan and our readiness to accept unknown opportunities with hopeful faith. We should develop gratitude while acknowledging God's current blessings, while expecting His future blessings to surpass all our expectations.

We should use our lives as proof of faith, which shines hope to those surrounding us. We should approach the future with absolute confidence because God provides sufficient grace, and His love never fails, while His plan for our lives remains perfect. The path to divine purpose may sometimes be difficult, but achieving life alignment with God's plan makes every obstacle worthwhile. Trust God's plan with complete faith and an open heart to discover how He will execute it through unexpected ways. Create a lifestyle that demonstrates the transformative power of following God's divine plan. Your hope should shine as a light in darkness, while your faith serves as a rock in turbulent times, and your love should guide those who surround you.

Through God's divine grace, the future contains numerous unspoken possibilities. Through embracing the journey and trusting in God's process, your life will develop as He guides it.

Chapter 30

The Theme Song

You can play or download the song for this book titled "The Path of True Direction" on Apple Music, Spotify, Amazon Music, YouTube Music, Tidal, Deezer, Pandora and almost every major music streaming service.

Acknowledgements

First and foremost, I want to thank you for reading this book. I'd really like to thank Doug Haynie for doing such a great job on my audiobook for me. Doug recorded the audiobook for The Great Gatsby. The novel is considered one of the greatest literary masterpieces of the 20th century, so I'm honored that Doug took on my project.

This book is dedicated to my wife, family and friends, whose unwavering support has been a constant source of encouragement and inspiration throughout my own journey. Their love and faith have been a beacon lighting my way during dark moments, reminding me of the profound truth that we are never truly alone. This book is a humble offering, a prayer of gratitude for the journey we have shared. It is a testament to grace's power, and a hope for a future where faith continues to guide our steps.